THE FIRST-YEAR
Seminar

Designing, Implementing, and Assessing Courses to Support Student Learning & Success

Designing and Administering the Course

Volume One

Jennifer R. Keup
and Joni Webb Petschauer

NATIONAL RESOURCE CENTER
FIRST-YEAR EXPERIENCE® AND STUDENTS IN TRANSITION
UNIVERSITY OF SOUTH CAROLINA

Cite as:

Keup, J. R., & Petschauer, J. W. (2011). *The first-year seminar: Designing, implementing, and assessing courses to support student learning and success: Vol. 1. Designing and administering the course.* Columbia, SC: University of South Carolina, National Resource Center for The First-Year Experience and Students in Transition.

Production Staff for the National Resource Center:

Series Editor	Tracy L. Skipper, Assistant Director for Publications
Design and Production	Melody Taylor, Graphic Artist

Additional copies of this book may be obtained from the National Resource Center for The First-Year Experience and Students in Transition, University of South Carolina, 1728 College Street, Columbia, SC 29208. Telephone (803) 777-6229. Fax (803) 777-4699.

Library of Congress Cataloging-in-Publication Data
Keup, Jennifer R.
   The first-year seminar : designing, implementing, and assessing courses to support student learning & success / Jennifer R. Keup and Joni Webb Petschauer.
       p. cm.
   Includes bibliographical references.
   ISBN 978-1-889271-75-0
   1. College freshmen--United States. 2. College student orientation--United States. 3. Interdisciplinary approach in education--United States. I. Petschauer, Joni Webb. II. Title.
   LB2343.32.K48 2011
   378.1'98--dc22
                          2011015354

Contents

List of Tables and Figures

Notes on the Series

The National Resource Center for The First-Year Experience and Students in Transition was founded in 1986 as an outgrowth of the first-year seminar (University 101) at the University of South Carolina and a national conference series that began as a discussion of the freshman seminar concept. Over the years, the Center's mission has expanded from a focus on a single course to the first college year to a range of transitions students may experience as they enter, make their way through, and move out of institutions of higher education. Yet, the Center continues to be housed within the University 101 program at the University of South Carolina, evidence of our ongoing connection and commitment to the first-year seminar as an invaluable learning experience for entering college students.

This commitment is also evidenced in the research activities, publications, and professional development events sponsored by the Center. Since the mid-1980s, the Center has conducted a triennial national survey examining the prevalence, structure, and administration of first-year seminars in American higher education. In 2010-2011, this research agenda expanded to examine the relationship between seminar characteristics and specific student outcomes. We have also contributed to a growing literature base about the efficacy of the seminar in promoting student learning, development, and retention in the first college year and beyond. To this end, we produced four volumes of campus-based research reports on the outcomes related to first-year seminars. And to date, more than 40 articles describing empirical research on first-year seminars have been published in the *Journal of The First-Year Experience & Students in Transition*. The First-Year Experience Monograph Series has included volumes on a research-based rationale for launching the course (Cuseo, 1991), faculty development for the seminar (Hunter & Skipper, 1999), using peer leaders in the course (Hamid, 2001), and embedding first-year seminars in learning communities (Henscheid, 2004). The Annual Conference on The First-Year Experience frequently features concurrent sessions and extended learning opportunities on select aspects of first-year seminar development and administration, and in recent years, the Center has hosted two institutes for first-year seminar leadership.

Despite this body of work, my colleagues at the Center and I frequently encounter educators—either new to the profession or new to first-year program leadership—who want more guidance on the design and launch of first-year seminars. The research and publications produced by the Center provide insight into how the courses are typically organized and offer a compelling rationale for why an institution might develop one, but they give little guidance on the myriad considerations that go into program design and institutionalization. As noted above, our publications have examined specific aspects of first-year seminars (e.g., faculty development, peer instruction), but the course has never been treated in its entirety. Finally, while the professional development events offered by the Center highlight the practical aspects of seminar administration, the nature of these events does not lend itself to a coherent, easily accessible discussion of practice.

To respond to this gap in the literature, my colleagues at the Center and I have developed a five-volume series on seminar design, implementation, administration, and assessment. One of the challenges in writing the series is that there is really no such thing as *the first-year seminar*. In reality, there are many first-year seminars, with different versions frequently co-existing on the same campus. Some seminars focus primarily on students' personal development and on their social and academic adjustment to college; others may look more like a traditional general education course taught in a small section where the instructor may emphasize academic skill development; and still others may offer interdisciplinary explorations of current or enduring issues while emphasizing the development of critical thinking and writing skills. As Jennifer Keup and Joni Petschauer note in this volume, decisions about the type or types of seminar to offer are driven by institutional culture, the characteristics of incoming students, and a host of other local factors. And the nature of the seminar will inform decisions about course goals, selection and training of instructors, content and pedagogy, and strategies for assessment. As such, this series does not offer a blueprint for designing and administering the first-year seminar as a specific course. Rather, it seeks to help readers see the possibilities for structuring first-year seminars in general and to offer some guidance on how to make choices among the various possibilities.

We also recognize that readers will come to this series at different points in their careers and at different points in the life cycle of a seminar. At its most basic level, the series is designed to offer new professionals or educators who are new to first-year program leadership with a crash course in seminar design and administration. However, it will also be useful to educators who are seeking ways to redesign a seminar program, to build in new components, or to enhance specific aspects of seminar administration. In this first volume, Keup and Petschauer outline the entire scope of seminar design and administration, drawing on what we know from national research and practice on individual campuses. Many of the issues discussed here, such as instructor recruitment and selection and course assessment, will be addressed in greater detail in later volumes, yet volume I offers a comprehensive discussion of the range of choices facing program leaders as they design (or redesign), administer, assess, and seek to sustain first-year seminars.

Volume II of the series, by Mary Stuart Hunter and James Groccia, will examine identifying and selecting instructors for the seminar, offer models for faculty development, and describe both content and pedagogies for faculty development initiatives. Building on this discussion, Brad Garner will examine teaching in the first-year seminar in volume III. Garner will describe the current population of college students and suggest how their characteristics coupled with what we know about effective teaching and learning should inform classroom practice. In addition to describing specific teaching strategies, Garner will also discuss course evaluation and assessment.

The Center's research on first-year seminars suggests that the use of peer instruction in the course is currently low (about 10% according to Tobolowsky & Associates, 2008). Yet, there is ample evidence to suggest the value of peer interactions in supporting the learning and adjustment of students in college (e.g., Astin, 1993; Pascarella & Terenzini, 1991). While less research exists on the impact of these experiences on peer leaders, a national study conducted by the National Resource Center in 2009 found that peer educators felt more connected to the institution and had more meaningful interactions with faculty and with their peers. About half of them reported that their academic performance improved as a result of their peer leadership experience (Keup & Mullins, 2010). It is our contention that the use of peers as mentors or co-instructors has the potential to greatly enhance the impact of the seminar. As such, volume IV, by Jennifer Latino and Michelle Ashcraft, will focus on incorporating peer education in the design and administration of the first-year seminar.

Throughout the series, the authors touch on assessing various aspects of the course—from implementing course evaluations and student self-assessments (volume III) to using course evaluations as a faculty development tool (volume II) to evaluating the impact of peer educators on the students in the course, on the peers themselves, and on the program (volume IV). Yet, given the increasing importance of measuring student learning and demonstrating program effectiveness, the series includes an entire volume on comprehensive program assessment. Dan Friedman concludes the series in volume V, offering a useful primer on assessment while tailoring the discussion to an examination of the first-year seminar.

We at the Center frequently encounter educators for whom the first-year experience is the first-year seminar. Yet, we take a much wider view, recognizing that the first-year experience is the sum total of the formal and informal academic and social encounters students have during their first year in higher education. On many campuses, implementing a first-year seminar may be the first step in the intentional design of a formal first-year experience. On others, a longstanding seminar is the signature event in the formal first-year experience, serving as a connecting point for other coursework, academic advising, and campus and civic engagement. At whatever point readers find the first-year seminar on their campuses, we hope this series will provide valuable insights for structuring courses that support individual student learning and success in the first college year.

Through the ongoing connection to the University 101 course at the University of South Carolina, many of the staff of the National Resource Center have direct experience in administering and teaching the first-year seminar. We have also had the opportunity to study its evolution in the higher education landscape and to learn from the countless educators in our network who have shared their own research and programmatic experiences with us over the years. So while I thank my colleagues at the University of South Carolina and elsewhere who served as authors for this series, I also want to acknowledge the contributions of members of the first-year experience and students in transition network. This network of educators and the students they serve provide the impetus for our work, but they also make it possible. As a reader of this series, you now are a part of this network. We welcome your feedback on this series and look forward to your own contributions to our collective knowledge about the first-year experience and other student transitions.

Tracy L. Skipper
Series Editor
National Resource Center for The First-Year Experience & Students in Transition
University of South Carolina

Overview

Colleges and universities seek to be dynamic and integrative learning communities that serve the needs of students and the aspirations of faculty in the context of an academic environment. First-year seminars have proven to be effective for addressing institutional challenges, from preparing students to navigate unknown futures, assisting faculty in discovering effective pedagogies, reinvigorating senior faculty through contact with a campus's newest members, providing insights into new curricula, and serving as a partner for initiatives as diverse as service-learning, residential learning communities, and undergraduate research.

This book is intended as a how-to guide for implementing or revising a first-year seminar. It provides faculty members and higher education administrators with a philosophical foundation, overview of fundamental elements, and set of practical guidelines needed when undertaking this task. In its most recent national triennial survey of campuses, the National Resource Center for The First-Year Experience and Students in Transition found that 87.3% of campuses reported having a first-year seminar (Padgett & Keup, in press). Moreover, the course existed in a variety of forms on all types of campuses (i.e., two- and four-year, public and private, large and small institutions). Despite differences among campus cultures and students served, there is both a core set of questions to consider when implementing any type of seminar program and the predictable need to make program modifications. This first volume, in a series of five, offers readers an essential handbook that includes a review of current literature and research, suggestions for a dynamic and sustainable implementation process, and campus-based examples of practice. Several topics introduced in this volume are more fully developed in subsequent ones. In particular, instructor selection and training as well as seminar assessment are fully independent volumes.

The authors developed each chapter as independent essays about the major components of a first-year seminar and as such, they can serve as individual field guides for committees or subgroups working to implement the course. The book provides a practical approach to launching and revising the seminar that can be adapted to virtually any campus because of an underlying appreciation and awareness of the academic environment in which the course must operate.

Chapter 1 provides a brief but fundamental history of first-year seminars and a working definition of the course as it is currently practiced on multiple campuses. It reviews a seminar typology, which demonstrates the breadth and flexibility of the course as campuses seek to address the needs of first-year students entering higher education. The review of the literature is enlivened by institutional profiles that detail a variety of successful seminars. All of these examples are punctuated by data from the 2006 National Survey of First-Year Seminars, which serve to identify common characteristics of different types of courses. Among the important elements the data address are seminar goals, structure, administration, pedagogy, content, instructors, and assessment strategies for various types of first-year seminars. The chapter concludes with a brief overview of important concepts necessary for the evaluation and selection of one or more seminar types.

Chapter 2 outlines the steps involved in launching the seminar over a 12-month period, including identifying a leadership team, designing the curriculum, recruiting and training instructors, marketing the course to students, and assessing its effectiveness. Specific tasks and timelines are suggested with an emphasis on developing broad-based campus input and long-term support. Recognizing that the seminar is only one component of a student's involvement with an institution, it is important for campuses to consider the course's role and its placement among various programs and initiatives to maximize the outcomes of all first-year programs individually and collectively.

Chapter 3 serves as a manual for course administration and addresses many of the challenges that come with initial implementation of a first-year seminar. Learning outcomes are addressed as they confirm the purpose and goals of the seminar. Course leadership, administrative location, and budgetary issues associated with the seminar are also discussed. Beyond this is a review of the organizational decisions that must be addressed on any campus, including (a) number of contact hours, (b) course size, (c) required versus the elective nature of the course, and (d) connection of the seminar to other institutional initiatives in the first college year. The chapter also provides a brief overview of instructor recruitment and training and some discussion about typical pedagogical approaches in these courses. The chapter concludes with recommendations for an assessment program for first-year seminars.

Chapter 4 invites the reader to consider the reasons for and reality of curricular and programmatic change. Respected faculty and administrative advocates often provide the heavy lifting when first-year seminars are initially implemented. The commitment and energy of these early adopters provide the resolve and reputation necessary to put the theory of first-year seminars into practice. However, the sustainability of a first-year seminar program relies on its ability to evolve over many decades and the impact of multiple personalities. This chapter provides an overview of commonly noted drivers for change, describes the difference between change and transition, and offers suggestions for managing the transition associated with change.

Chapter 5 identifies some important guidelines and themes for ensuring effectiveness and moving toward excellence with respect to the first-year seminar. The concluding chapter points to common elements in first-year college success models that provide a foundation launching, administering, refining, and sustaining a seminar and identifies some general best practices that pave the way to continual success for the course. Further, the chapter contextualizes first-year seminars within a larger framework of initiatives for an integrated and comprehensive first-year experience and educational trajectory through college and beyond.

The book also includes two appendices: (a) a list of resources, of which first-year seminar administrators and instructors need a working knowledge, and (b) a list of first-year seminar assessment resources. Listservs, publications, associations and centers, and professional development opportunities (e.g., manuals, conferences, workshops) are provided with abbreviated descriptions and websites for additional information when available. Without a doubt, the National Resource Center for The First-Year Experience and Students in Transition on the campus of the University of South Carolina is the heart of the modern first-year seminar in the United States. The Center provides an invaluable service as a national clearinghouse for resources and research associated with the seminar from a number of different colleges, research centers, grant-funded initiatives, organizations, and associations within higher education. Further, Center staff and its interactive website of first-year resources can assist educators with identifying individuals and institutions engaged in innovative practice.

The responsibility for leading curricular revision is an ever-evolving role that requires an administrator to adapt and build upon skills in order to meet new challenges and expectations. This book identifies institutions across the country with seminars in a variety of forms and stages of development that can serve as models or resources for additional research, visits, or calls when approaching a particularly thorny problem or issue. Readers should allow the campus stories in this book to inspire connections among administrators, collaboration among institutions, and communication among practitioners about the uniqueness and universality of the first-year seminar.

Chapter 1
Introducing the First-Year Seminar

Millions of students enter the halls of higher education institutions as first-time, full-time students each academic year. Further, enrollment in higher education institutions is expected to grow and diversify, especially in the coming decade, with respect to student backgrounds; levels of academic preparation; mental, emotional, and physical health care needs; and expectations for college (Crissman Ishler, 2005; National Center for Education Statistics, 2009; Pryor, Hurtado, DeAngelo, Palucki Blake, & Tran, 2009; Western Interstate Commission for Higher Education, 2008). Despite their differences, all students will go through the process of adjusting to their new lives as college students.

Statistics about college student satisfaction, success, and persistence paint a somber picture with respect to students' successful transition into and through the first year of college. Data from the American College Testing (2009, 2010) service show that persistence to the second year is on a decline, with only two thirds of students returning to college after their first year. Further, national data indicate that first-year students are studying only about half as much as faculty say is necessary to be successful in their classes, are underutilizing support services and staff, are working more hours than is optimal for their academic experience, and are managing more profound mental and emotional health care needs during their adjustment than ever before (Crissman Ishler, 2005; Gallagher, 2004; Liu, Sharkness, & Pryor, 2008; NSSE, 2009). These statistics provide strong evidence that many students struggle during their transition to college.

In light of these findings, colleges and universities have developed many programs and practices to facilitate students' adjustment to college; personal and academic success; and, ultimately, persistence to the second year and beyond. Examples of these efforts include orientation programs; peer leadership, education, and mentoring; campus-sponsored welcome activities; workshops and tutorials (focused on personal and academic skills); residential life programming; as well as new pedagogies and courses. While many of these programs have found a home in the cocurriculum, there has also been a renewed interest in the classroom and coursework as a "gateway for student involvement in the academic and social communities of a college" (Braxton, Milem, & Sullivan, 2000, p. 570). In truth, the classroom remains the one common forum where students may be reached, a point that is even more important given that numerous forces draw today's students away from cocurricular involvement. These forces include the facts that more than 20% of entering students at four-year institutions and nearly all students at two-year colleges do not live on campus; nearly one third of first-year students at least occasionally feel that family responsibilities interfere with schoolwork; the proportion of part-time and nontraditional students has increased significantly in the past few decades; and the percentage of students expecting to work at least part-time, if not full-time, while in college has increased 10 percentage points over the past 20 years (Crissman Ishler, 2005; Liu et al., 2008; Pryor et al., 2009; Pryor, Hurtado, Saenz, Santos, & Korn, 2007). One of the most prominent curricular programs being used to assist students in their transition from high school to college and to enhance the social and academic integration of new students is the first-year seminar.

This chapter begins the in-depth exploration into the processes of developing and delivering high-quality first-year seminars that will be addressed further in this volume and in the entire book series on this topic. As a foundation for this ongoing discussion, the current chapter offers a brief history and working definition for first-year seminars. It then differentiates these courses by introducing a commonly used typology for first-year seminars and draws upon the results of national surveys and institutional profiles of successful seminars to identify and illustrate common characteristics of various types of these courses. More specifically, these data provide important details about seminar goals, structure, administration, pedagogy, content, instructors, and assessment strategies for different types of first-year seminars, thus providing a resource for educators to learn about, implement, refine, and research this widely used curricular intervention. These portraits of typical practices for each seminar type are not meant to minimize the rich diversity of seminars within each category. Instead, they are intended to provide a general understanding of various seminar offerings as a guide for the reader to navigate the content of this volume and book series. The chapter concludes with a brief overview of some important concepts to help evaluate these seminar types and characteristics and guide the careful consideration and selection of first-year seminars on an institutional level.

Background and Definition of First-Year Seminars

First-year seminars are far from a recent innovation in postsecondary education, and, in fact, have their roots in the late 19th century. Early first-year seminars emerged in the late 1800s, most notably at Lee College in Kentucky in 1882 and Boston College in 1888 (Barefoot & Fidler, 1996; Gahagan, 2002; Saunders & Romm, 2008). These courses were used as an extended orientation to the institution, to fulfill the institution's responsibility to act in loco parentis, and to aid in the students' social adjustment and academic development. The popularity and use of these courses waxed and waned over the 20th century until they all but died out by the 1960s when the era of in loco parentis ended, faculty became disenchanted with teaching the life-skills content of the courses, and a sink-or-swim attitude became more of the norm toward student success (Saunders & Romm).

Several factors converged in the 1970s that led to a resurgence of interest in first-year seminars, including enormous growth in the overall pool of college-aged students in the post-World War II Baby Boom generation; changes in legislation and financial aid policies that increased access to higher education for previously underrepresented populations of students; and, likely a correlate to increased access, a larger population of underprepared students who were struggling to be successful in higher education (Cohen & Kisker, 2010; Koch & Gardner, 2006; Saunders & Romm, 2008). Higher education then rediscovered first-year seminars as an important tool in the effort to facilitate the success of entering college students and to enhance first-to-second-year retention rates among the general population of entering students and particularly among academically underprepared, first-generation, and historically underrepresented students. Today, as many as 94% of accredited four-year colleges and universities in the United States offer a first-year seminar to at least some students, and more than half offer a first-year seminar to 90% or more of their first-year students. National data indicate that these courses are present on a small, but significant, proportion of two-year colleges as well (Barefoot, 2002; Tobolowsky & Associates, 2008).

While first-year seminars can take a variety of forms, Barefoot (1992) offers the following definition in her comprehensive report of national survey research on first-year seminars:

> The freshman seminar is a course intended to enhance the academic and/or social integration of first-year students by introducing them (a) to a variety of specific topics, which vary by seminar type, (b) to essential skills for college success, and (c) to selected processes, the most common of which is the creation of a peer support group. (p. 49)

Barefoot, along with her research colleague Paul P. Fidler (1996), also identified criteria of successful first-year seminars, which include

> courses that are 1) offered for academic credit; 2) are centered in the first-year curriculum; 3) involve both faculty and student affairs professionals in a program design and instruction; 4) include instructor training and development as an integral part of the program; 5) compensate or otherwise reward instructors for teaching the seminar; 6) involve upper-level students in seminar delivery; and 7) include ways of assessing their effectiveness and disseminating these assessments to the campus community. (qtd. in Hunter & Linder, 2005, p. 277)

Based upon this definition and conditions for success, an extensive literature base describing outcomes related to first-year seminars has emerged. Indeed, the first-year seminar may be the most researched course in the undergraduate curriculum (Koch, 2001; Koch, Foote, Hinkle, Keup & Pistilli, 2007; Tobolowsky, Cox, & Wagner, 2005). In short, this research has established the first-year seminar as one of the most important instructional vehicles for achieving the learning and developmental objectives of undergraduate education in the United States. The bulk of these studies have examined the impact of the course on retention, persistence to graduation, and academic performance (e.g., Barefoot, Warnock, Dickinson, Richardson, & Roberts, 1998; Bedford & Durkee, 1989; Cavote & Kopera-Frye, 2004; Cuseo, 1991; Fidler, 1991; Fidler & Moore, 1996; Schnell & Doetkott, 2002-3; Tinto, 1993). However, other studies have indicated the positive effects of first-year seminar participation on a range of other outcomes such as involvement in campus activities (Starke, Harth, & Sirianni, 2001); interaction with faculty (Hopkins, 1988; Keup & Barefoot, 2005; Maisto & Tammi, 1991); student engagement (Kuh, 2005); and improvement of students' skills in problem solving, critical reading, writing, and general study behaviors (Barefoot et al., 1998; Tobolowsky et al.). Teacher preparation workshops associated with seminars have also been linked to improved teaching performance for faculty, including the use of engaging pedagogies in the seminar and in other courses (Barefoot, et al., 1998; Fidler, Neururer-Rotholz, & Richardson, 1999; Tobolowsky et al.). Summing up this research Pascarella and Terenzini (2005) suggest, "FYS [first-year seminar] participation has statistically significant and substantial, positive effects on a student's successful transition to college and the likelihood of persistence into the second year as well as on academic performance while in college" (p. 403).

The documented success of first-year seminars has led them to become the curricular cornerstone of many first-year experience programs. In fact, they are so often the foundation of institutional support for new students that the phrase the *first-year experience* is commonly misused in reference to a seminar rather than to an "intentional combination of academic and co-curricular efforts within and across postsecondary institutions" (Koch & Gardner, 2006, p. 2). While not in and of itself a first-year experience, these seminars are often used in combination with service-learning initiatives, learning communities, residential life, peer mentoring, common reading programs, and academic advising for new students. As such, first-year seminars have become one of the most common elements of first-year experience programs across the country and are often the natural next step for new students after orientation.

Types and Characteristics of First-Year Seminars

While first-year seminars vary greatly, there are some general structural commonalities. National data show that the vast majority of these courses last one full term (either semester or quarter), are offered for academic credit toward graduation, are offered for a letter grade, and maintain smaller class sizes (e.g., 16-24 students) in line with their seminar status (Hunter & Linder, 2005; Tobolowsky & Associates, 2008). However, numerous other factors differ by institutional type, control, context, and mission. In order to better understand this course, its administration, and associated outcomes in a way that is less institutionally bound, Barefoot (1992) identified a general typology of first-year seminars that is still largely used today. According to her early research on these courses, five basic types exist: (a) the extended orientation seminar, which provides general academic support and an introduction to campus resources; (b) an academic seminar with uniform content across all sections; (c) an academic seminar with thematic sections (i.e., variable content); (d) a preprofessional or discipline-linked seminar, which frequently serves as an introduction to a major;

and (e) a basic study skills seminar to support academically underprepared students. Subsequent research on the seminar revealed that such courses are especially malleable, with schools combining elements of different types of seminars to develop a hybrid seminar uniquely designed to support the institutional mission and "the growing needs of a changing student demographic" (Gahagan, 2002, p. 6; Tobolowsky & Associates, 2008). Data from of the 2006 National Survey of First-Year Seminars, administered by the National Resource Center for The First-Year Experience and Students in Transition, will be used to provide a portrait of first-year seminar by course type (Tobolowsky & Associates).

Extended Orientation

Extended orientation first-year seminars are both the most common and the type with the longest history. The earliest identified examples of first-year seminars were of this type, and national data show that 57.9% of colleges and universities offer an extended orientation seminar and approximately 40% offer it as their primary seminar type. As stated above, these seminars primarily "focus on student survival and success techniques" (Hunter & Linder, 2005, p. 279). National survey data show that the three most important course objectives reported for institutions with extended orientation seminars as their primary type were orientation to campus resources and services, development of academic skills, and encouragement of self-exploration and personal development.

Definitions of and approaches to *success* and *survival* are sure to change by institutional context, characteristics, and mission. For instance, Abilene Christian University (Abilene, TX), a small, private, four-year college, states that their extended orientation seminar "strives to build community; explore campus heritage and culture; provide career, academic, and personal advice; teach study skills; and confirm a major" in an effort to "teach college success skills and ease the transition to college life" (Tobolowsky et al., 2005, p. 9). Northern Kentucky University (Highland Heights, KY), a midsized, public four-year institution, represents another approach by designing their extended orientation course around just two guiding questions: "What do students need to know and do in order to be successful in their first college year?" and "When do they need to know and do it?" (Tobolowsky et al., pp. 107-108). These questions yield a set of 10 outcomes that are common across all sections of the course and focus on the exploration of self, community, and campus resources. In yet another example, the University of North Carolina at Charlotte uses a strengths-based and team-building approach in their first-year seminar to "provide students with information and tools that will help them gain a better awareness of campus resources and services, encourage them to get connected to the university community, and enhance strategies for successful academic and personal growth" (Tobolowsky et al., pp. 176-177).

Extended orientation courses are more frequently represented at larger campuses, public institutions, as well as less selective colleges and universities. Along with basic study skills courses, they are one of only two types of first-year seminars that have a significant presence on two-year campuses; more than three quarters of two-year institutions in the 2006 National Survey of First-Year Seminars reported having this type of seminar, and 60% of this same institutional subsample indicated that this was their primary type of first-year seminar. Given that large, public, and two-year institutions often have reputations for depersonalized student experiences, it is encouraging to see these colleges and universities using first-year seminars as a way to overcome these institutional challenges and forge a connection with new students.

Despite their popularity nationally, extended orientation seminars tend to be offered for less academic credit than other seminar types. Just under two thirds of institutions reporting data on this first-year seminar type indicated that it was a one-credit seminar, which is more than double the rate of any other seminar type. Further, only one third of these same respondents indicated that their extended orientation course contributed toward general education credit, and one half reported that these credits were applicable only as an elective. Additionally, perhaps again due to institutional size and bureaucracy, only about one third of institutions responding to the 2006 National Survey of First-Year Seminars reported that extended orientation courses were required. However, a slightly higher percentage of these respondents indicated that the seminar was required of provisionally admitted students than institutions reporting about other types of first-year seminars.

Although survey data show that faculty and academic administrators had a strong role in the extended orientation course, student affairs professionals were more often represented in the administration and delivery of extended orientation courses than for any other type. Most notably, nearly two thirds of institutions with extended orientation courses reported that student affairs professionals had teaching responsibilities in the course—a rate that is a full 20 to 50 percentage-points higher than responses from any other first-year seminar type. Moreover, any faculty who taught this type of first-year seminar most often did so outside their regular teaching load. Further, these data showed that the administrative home of extended orientation first-year seminars was slightly less likely than other seminar types to reside in academic affairs or an academic department and was more frequently found in student affairs. Finally, if the director or dean of extended orientation first-year seminars had another campus role, it was more often as a student affairs administrator than for other seminar types.

As compared to other types of first-year seminars, extended orientation courses were more likely to report study skills, campus resources, academic planning and advising, and relationship issues as the most important course topics. They were similar to basic study skills courses in their more frequent coverage of time management skills and college policies and procedures than to academic, preprofessional, or hybrid first-year seminars. Conversely, institutions with extended orientation courses were far less likely to report addressing specific disciplinary topics, writing skills, and critical thinking than those with other primary seminars types. It is not surprising that extended orientation courses reported assessment activities for a greater number of outcomes than other seminar types, but most notably increased persistence to the sophomore year, enhanced student connection with peers, and greater use of campus services.

Academic

The primary focus of academic first-year seminars is "on [an] academic theme/discipline but [they] will often include academic skills components such as critical thinking or expository writing" (Saunders & Romm, 2008, p. 2). Academic seminars typically take two forms: (a) ones with generally uniform content across sections and (b) those in which the content varies based upon section and instructor. Although extended orientation courses have been, and remain, the most common type of first-year seminars, academic seminars with uniform content and those with variable content have maintained the second and third spots, respectively. In fact, when combined, the percent of institutions reporting that they offer an academic seminar has increased by more than two and half times the rate at which they were reported on the 1991 National Survey of First-Year Seminars and are now within 10 percentage points of the rate of offering reported for extended orientation courses (Tobolowsky & Associates, 2008). Given the increasing proportion of students entering college with lower levels of academic achievement in high school, decreasing levels of time spent studying, and reports of high school grade inflation during this same time period (Pryor et al., 2007), it is likely that the popularity of academic seminars is the result of higher education's efforts to offset an increasingly academically disengaged population of first-year students. In effect, academic first-year seminars represent a valuable tool to introduce students to college-level scholarship and assist them in their adjustment to the life of the mind expected of them as college undergraduates.

Examples of this emphasis can be seen in the purpose statements of various academic seminars. For example, the University of Bridgeport (Bridgeport, CT), a small, private, four-year college, uses their academic seminar with uniform content to "help students understand the academic culture at the University and to provide a context for adoption of this academic culture" (Tobolowsky et al., 2005, p. 155). While vastly different in enrollment (it is five times larger than the University of Bridgeport) and control (public vs. private), Southwest Missouri State University (Springfield, MO) includes similar goals in the mission statement of its academic seminar with uniform content: "The mission of the course is to facilitate the transition to university life and assist students in achieving academic success [by presenting] opportunities for students to... explore the academic environment at the university" (Tobolowsky et al., p. 140).

While generally similar in focus, academic seminars with variable content tend to capitalize on faculty members' areas of expertise and interest to create an introduction to collegiate academics via interdisciplinary approaches and critical inquiry. For example, first-year students at the University of Colorado at Colorado Springs, a midsized, public, four-year university, may select among "eight multiple-section, thematic, first-year courses...created by cross-college teams of three to five faculty" on topics that range from a focus on Colorado Living to Life and Death to one titled Mating Game (Tobolowsky et al., p. 163). Wheaton College (Norton, MA), a small, private four-year institution, created an academic seminar with variable content in which "each section is built around a topic that reflects the instructor's choice of a controversial theme or issue related to his/her area of expertise" in order to "hone important skills needed to succeed in college" such as critical thinking, academic inquiry, and communication skills (Tobolowsky et al., p. 183).

National data show that developing academic skills is among the top three course objectives for both types of academic first-year seminars. Another important goal for academic seminars with uniform content is creating a common first-year experience. According to 2006 national data, approximately 60% of respondents with this as their primary seminar ranked the common experience as among their most important course objectives (Tobolowsky & Associates, 2008). In fact, it exceeded the ranking for extended orientation seminars on this goal by more than 30 percentage points. For academic seminars with variable content, increasing student-faculty interaction was the second most highly rated course outcome after developing academic skills. Creating a common first-year experience ranked third. In support of these goals, both types of academic seminars were more likely to highlight critical thinking in course content than other types of seminars and included a heavier emphasis on writing skills. Given their connection with faculty areas of interest, it is not surprising that a specific focus on a disciplinary topic was a higher priority content area for academic seminars with variable content than for academic seminars with uniform content. However, it is interesting to note that academic courses with variable content actually ranked this content area even higher than respondents with preprofessional first-year seminars, thus suggesting that the content of academic seminars may be more embedded in the disciplines than their preprofessional counterparts (Tobolowsky & Associates, 2008).

With respect to institutional characteristics, academic first-year seminars tend to be offered at private institutions more frequently than at public colleges and universities are overrepresented at four-year institutions. Further, academic seminars with variable content are three or more times more likely than any other type of first-year seminar to be found at institutions with high selectivity and are slightly more common at institutions with over 20,000 students.

Within these institutional environments, it is also interesting to note how these types of seminars are typically structured. Academic first-year seminars of both types tended to have a class size of 16-20 students, which is similar to preprofessional first-year seminars and slightly smaller than other types of first-year seminars. Further, these courses were significantly more likely to be required of all first-year students than any other type of first-year seminar, were uniformly offered for academic credit toward graduation, and tended to be three-credit classes. Similar to all types of first-year seminars, academic courses were most often one-term (i.e., quarter or semester) long, although approximately 17% of institutions reporting that academic seminars with uniform content was their primary seminar type indicated that the course was a year long, nearly double the reported rate of any other type of first-year seminar (Tobolowksy & Associates, 2008). Finally, with respect to particular curricular components, both types of academic seminars tended to incorporate online components and learning communities at rates similar to those of other seminar types, but academic courses with variable content used service-learning and team teaching at a slightly higher rate than extended orientation and academic courses with uniform content and significantly more than basic study skills seminars.

Unlike extended orientation courses, the majority of academic first-year seminars were housed in academic affairs. According to national data for institutions where academic first-year seminars were the primary type, a dean, director, or coordinator was typically designated for the course, but it was more frequently a part-time position that was taken on by a faculty member than for any other type of first-year seminar. Further, faculty members were almost uniformly involved in teaching responsibilities for academic seminars, which were most often counted toward their regular teaching load rather than an overload.

Basic Study Skills

As the name implies, basic study skills first-year seminars are intended to support academically underprepared students in their transition to college. The focus of these types of seminars is on "basic academic skills such as grammar, note taking, and reading texts" (Tobolowsky & Associates, 2008, p. 106). For example, California State University, San Marcos, a medium-sized, public, four-year university, offers a basic study skills course that includes topics such as "time management, study skills, oral presentation skills, career development, library information and research, and health and wellness" (Tobolowsky et al., 2005, p. 33). Similarly, Northern Illinois University (DeKalb, IL), a large, public, four-year institution, also offers a basic study skills course with similar content as well as a focus on "students' academic and social adjustment to college" (p. 103). Miami Dade College (Miami, FL), a large, public, community college, offers a basic study skills seminar where the goals include "supporting the student in transition, shaping success strategies and attitudes, forming lifelong learning skills,... developing personal awareness and emotional intelligence,... information literacy, and technology skills" (Griffin & Romm, 2008, pp. 49-50).

Institutions that reported basic study skills courses as their primary type of first-year seminar overwhelmingly indicated that the development of study skills was the most important course topic. Other important course topics included time management and academic planning or advising, and approximately one third of institutional respondents to the 2006 National Survey of First-Year Seminars reported that campus resources, career exploration or preparation, and critical thinking were important course topics. Conversely, these classes very rarely prioritized diversity issues, relationship issues, or college policies and procedures in their course content. Interestingly, despite the fact that academic performance is often embedded in a major or disciplinary perspective, a minority of these courses reported covering specific disciplinary topics.

Similarly surprising given students' challenges with writing at a college level (Beil & Knight, 2007; Sanoff, 2006), fewer than 10% of institutions reporting basic study skills as their primary seminar type indicate that writing skills are a focus of their course content.

Given the increased attention both nationally and within higher education on issues related to college readiness, remediation, developmental education, and academically underprepared students (Crissman Ishler, 2005; Duranczyk & White, 2003; NSSE, 2008; Pryor et al., 2009), it is not surprising that the proportion of institutions that report offering these courses has increased nearly four-fold in the past few decades: from 6% in 1991 to approximately 22% currently, although only 6% reported that this is their primary seminar type on the 2006 National Survey of First-Year Seminars (Tobolowsky & Associates, 2008). Basic study skills courses are disproportionately represented at two-year colleges, at less selective institutions, and among public colleges and universities although they are fairly evenly represented across categories of institutional size.

Like other types of seminars, basic study skills seminars were most often offered for one semester or quarter and carried academic credit toward graduation. Similar to extended orientation courses, they had slightly higher class sizes (between 16 and 25), were more likely to assign grades of pass/fail rather than letter grades, and had similar rates of faculty participation in course instruction (approximately 85%). However, basic study skills courses also had some significant differences from all other seminars types. For example, basic study skills were significantly less likely to be required of all students than any other seminar type and were, instead, more often required of provisionally admitted students. Further, these seminars tended to be offered for more credit hours than other types with as much as half of them offered for three credits. However, credits for basic skills seminars were counted as an elective rather than as a general education requirement much more frequently than for other first-year seminar types. These seminars were also unique with respect to their use of curricular tools and strategies. Most notably, these types of first-year seminars were slightly less likely to be linked to other courses (i.e., learning community structure), were overrepresented in online-only sections, and were significantly less likely (i.e., less than 10%) to incorporate a service-learning component or team-teaching. Finally, basic study skills were much less likely to offer and require instructor training for the courses; in fact, rates of instructor training were approximately half that for other types of seminars.

Unlike other seminar types, the administrative home for basic study skills courses was virtually nonexistent in first-year program offices and tended to be evenly distributed across academic affairs, academic departments, and to a somewhat lesser degree, student affairs. In other words, basic study skills were not generally owned by a common unit on campus. Perhaps because of this lack of uniformity, only about half of institutions with basic study skills seminars reported having a dean, director, or coordinator, which was significantly lower than for extended orientation courses or either type of academic first-year seminar. Further, only about half of these positions were full-time with the majority of these part-time professionals also maintaining an academic affairs position in addition to their oversight of the course.

According to national data, the most important outcomes identified for basic study skills courses were to develop academic skills, orient students to campus resources and services, and encourage self-exploration or personal development. While institutions that offered basic study skills seminars were less likely to report on course assessment, except evaluation of institutional data, than other seminars, almost two thirds attributed persistence to the sophomore year as a result of the basic study skills course; and just under half identified enhanced academic abilities as the result of the course. Both of these success rates were higher than similar reports for any other first-year seminar type.

Preprofessional

Similar to how extended orientation seminars introduce new students to the university and academic seminars serve as an orientation to the life of the mind at the college level, preprofessional first-year seminars are typically used to introduce students to a specific major, discipline, and/or profession. In other words, these types of first-year seminars serve as a means of transitioning not only to college but also to the larger community of a discipline and career. They are generally offered within "professional schools or academic disciplines such as engineering, health sciences, business, or education," and data from the 2006 National Survey of First-Year Seminars show that developing academic skills, introduction to a discipline, and creating a common first-year experience were ranked highest among the most important course objectives for preprofessional seminars, while encouragement of arts participation and retention to the sophomore year were the lowest (Tobolowsky & Associates, 2008, p. 106). For instance, Castleton State College (Castleton, VT), a small, four-year, public college, "offers a variety of discipline-linked seminars such as Introduction to History of Art, Principles of Computer Information Systems, and Basic Musicianship" (Hunter & Linder, 2005, p. 280). In another example, the University of South Carolina Columbia, a large, four-year, public university, offers major-specific versions of their first-year seminar course in journalism, education, and exercise science.

In 2006, approximately 14% of institutions reported offering this type of seminar, which is 10 times the rate at which these courses were reported in 1991. Nearly 4% of institutions indicated that preprofessional first-year courses are the seminar type with the greatest enrollment on the National Survey of First-Year Seminars; thus, these seminars were less likely to be the primary seminar than any other seminar type. Because of the smaller number of institutions offering it as their primary seminar, reliable data, trends, and issues with respect to this type of seminar are more difficult to determine. For example, although preprofessional or discipline-linked courses are offered at a slightly higher rate at private institutions as compared to their public counterparts, analyses of national data did not yield any other significant differences by institutional size, type, enrollment, or selectivity.

In course structure, national data indicated that preprofessional first-year seminars were similar to other types in their one-term duration, high level of letter grading, and tendency to carry three credit hours toward graduation. However, the structure and characteristics of preprofessional first-year seminars did have some statistical and practical differences from other types of seminars. For example, these courses tended to be slightly smaller than other types with a much greater frequency reporting a class size ranging from 16 to 20 students. Further, they were required of all students at a much lower rate than other types of seminars but, in line with their purpose, were much more often required of students within specific majors and had the course credit applied to students' majors. In fact the degree to which preprofessional seminars were required of students in a specific major—75% of institutions reporting that preprofessional seminars have the highest enrollment also indicated this requirement—represented the highest rate of requirement for any student subpopulation for any type of first-year seminar (Tobolowsky & Associates, 2008). Preprofessional first-year seminars were similar to other types in that their administrative home is on the academic side of the institution (academic affairs or academic department) and in high rates of faculty involvement in teaching the course. However, perhaps due to their lower levels of requirement and their topical connection to specific disciplines and majors, institutional respondents also reported the lowest rates of having a dedicated dean, director, or coordinator for this type of course when compared to other first-year seminars.

Instruction and pedagogical approaches also represent an area of uniqueness for preprofessional first-year seminars. Career exploration, critical thinking, specific disciplinary topics, and academic planning or advising were among the highest-ranked course topics while relationship issues, diversity issues, and writing skills were the lowest-ranked course topics for these seminars. Data from institutions reporting that preprofessional seminars had the highest enrollment on their campus indicated that these courses used online components at a slightly lower rate than other types of seminars. However, these same data also showed that preprofessional seminars were among the highest in their use of service-learning, were much more likely to use team-teaching strategies, used undergraduate and graduate student teachers at a higher rate, and were more likely to include the first-year seminar in a learning community structure than other types of seminars.

So few institutions indicating that preprofessional or discipline-linked seminars were their primary seminar type on the 2006 National Survey of First-Year Seminars provided evidence of assessment and evaluation of these courses that analyses of these practices could not be performed.[1] As such, no assessment practices were reported for these courses for that survey administration. While it is always preferable to have specific information, in this case, the absence of findings also lends support to certain conclusions, most notably that the rate of assessment of preprofessional and discipline-linked first-year seminars needs to increase. Such assessment data would certainly be useful in examinations of national trends. However, even more important, assessment of these courses and effective use of those findings would help enhance their delivery, content, and impact on an institutional level. While other findings from analyses of national data on preprofessional seminars suggest impediments to such assessment activities (e.g., greater use for specialized populations, least likely to be used as a primary seminar, few instances of a dedicated leadership position), in an era of increased accountability in higher education, it is ever more critical to collect, report, and use assessment information to ensure the sustainability of preprofessional and discipline-linked courses.

---

[1] In order to protect institutional confidentiality, when specific data analyses yielded fewer than 10 cases, the data were omitted from the report of findings.

Considerations for Selecting a Seminar Type

These definitions and types of first-year seminars have generally withstood the test of time. However, the evolution of first-year seminars as a curricular intervention has also introduced a degree of complexity as institutions use multiple types of first-year seminars and blend these types into hybrid courses. In fact, recent national data indicate that nearly three quarters of institutions reported offering more than one type of first-year seminar and well over half indicate that special sections of the seminar are offered for certain sub-populations of students at their campuses (Padgett & Keup, in press; Tobolowsky & Associates, 2008). Further, approximately one quarter of respondents to the 2006 National Survey of First-Year Seminars offered a course that did not fit within the categories listed above and indicated that they offered a hybrid or other type of first-year seminar (Tobolowsky & Associates). These trends of offering multiple types of first-year seminars and increased flexibility within the typology can be seen as positive developments in the first-year experience and students in transition movement, especially because selecting the *right* type of course can seem like a daunting task and is typically a point at which institutions perseverate in their process of considering and implementing a first-year seminar. While there is some research that indicates a relationship between seminar type and learning outcomes (Friedman & Marsh, 2009; Swing, 2002), the selection of course type is less about a search for a right answer and more about finding the best fit for student needs and institutional goals in service to students.

At the core of this process is a focus on student-centeredness. Student-centered learning is an approach to focusing on the needs of the student rather than needs of others involved in the process, such as teachers and administrators. This approach to learning is recommended because it suggests that institutional leadership, staff, and course instructors focus on the strengths and weaknesses of first-year students, placing their learning outcomes at the forefront of the resources offered and the course material presented. The teacher serves as an active facilitator of learning rather than the bearer of knowledge. Individual students, classmates, instructors, and/or student and professional members of the campus community share in the evaluation of learning (Braxton et al., 2000; Pascarella & Terenzini, 2005).

The first-year seminar lends itself to a student-centered approach. The course covers a certain amount of universal content, but it is most often about the individual student's ability to identify a path of educational success within the context of a specific academic community. Obviously, the implications for the design of curriculum, course content, and pedagogy are significant and should support a student-centered focus. Regardless of the course type and structure, in- and out-of-class activities and assignments should provide opportunities for students to demonstrate their understanding of how to use campus resources to support their educational journey. In order for the students to be fully engaged as a partner in the process of their adjustment, learning, and success, multiple opportunities for self-reflection and self-monitoring with regards to student development and change need to be embedded in the course framework (Baxter Magolda, 1999; Engberg & Mayhew, 2007). Irrespective of course type and approach, fundamentally the first-year seminar is more of a process course than a product course. The goal of the instructor is to help the student engage in an integrity-filled discovery process that can be used time and time again. Students must not only identify how they learn but also integrate that awareness into their educational identity. By contrast, a course that is content-centered might cover topics and use teaching methods considered irrelevant by the student. And, a course that is instructor-centered would emphasis the instructor's intellectual preferences and strengths (Weimer, 2002). The case can be made for any of these approaches in a variety of courses, but all first-year seminars are fundamentally courses about student success. As such, it makes the most sense to focus on the student in the process of selecting the right course for an institution.

Beyond a student-centered approach, a few other concepts can help guide the process of finding the seminar type that provides the greatest degree of alignment for an institution and the students it serves. Two of the most notable concepts—knowledge of student characteristics and understanding of institutional culture—are described in greater detail below.

Knowledge of Student Characteristics and Needs

Shared knowledge of the characteristics and expectations of the students at an institution as well as what they need to assist them in their transition into and through higher education is critical to the identification of the appropriate type of course and successful administration of a first-year seminar. This understanding of student needs is likely to include an in-depth institutional analysis of student-level data, such as background (e.g., race, ethnicity, gender, first-generation student status), academic preparation, first-year challenges, retention rates, use of student services and campus resources, proportion of students who are undeclared or change majors in the first year, and courses with the highest failure and withdrawal rates. It is also useful to evaluate these data within the context of historical trends (e.g., How do these students compare to previous cohorts of students?), peer institutions (e.g., How do campus statistics compare to similar data points from peer institutions?), and even aspirational benchmarks (e.g., How do institutional data compare to aspirant universities or standards of best practice?).

In order to be truly student-centered in institutional approach and in the administration of a first-year seminar, it is critical to be open and honest about students' strengths and challenges. Too often educators fall into the trap of focusing on the students that they wish they had or used to have rather than ones that they currently serve. Additionally, being student-centered requires the consideration of the unique educational challenges and developmental opportunities that are representative of certain student subpopulations. While an understanding of students in the aggregate is efficient, it can often overlook the concerns, issues, and characteristics of specific student groups that could gain the most from specialized attention. In fact, higher education researchers argue for more specialized understanding of student subpopulations and the differential impact of student success initiatives on these groups of undergraduates (Cronbach & Snow, 1977; Pascarella, 2006; Pascarella & Terenzini, 1991). For example, Pascarella states that "academic and out-of-class experiences that influence intellectual and personal development during college differ along such dimensions as race/ethnicity...and first-generation versus non-first generation status" as well as gender, major, socioeconomic status, academic preparation, and a host of other student features (p. 512). As such, it becomes critical to collect and interpret student data on institutionally salient subgroups as well as in the aggregate.

In sum, a current, accurate, and nuanced understanding of student needs is likely to suggest a fit between those issues and the purposes and common objectives of a specific seminar type, or several different types, to address the needs of first-year undergraduates as well as different subpopulations of students.

An Understanding of Institutional Culture and Goals

The other influential factors to consider during decisions about which seminar(s) to offer and how to administer them are institutional culture and goals. While institutional culture and student characteristics are often highly correlated, it is important to understand culture as its own force since it is typically what attracts students, staff, and faculty to an institution. Moreover, it is a discernable factor in students' satisfaction and success in an institutional environment, motivates resource decisions, and is likely reflected in institutional mission and strategic goals. Kuh and Whitt (1988) defined culture in American colleges and universities as "persistent patterns of norms, values, practices, beliefs, and assumptions that shape the behavior of individuals and groups in a college or university and provide a frame of reference within which to interpret the meaning of events and actions on and off the campus" (p. iv). It is often difficult to determine because it includes "unconscious, taken-for-granted...perceptions, thoughts, and feelings" as well as espoused strategies, identified goals, and "visible organizational structures" (Schein, 1992, p. 17). However, an honest examination of institutional culture is important as cultural congruence will be critical to the success of any initiative offered therein, including a first-year seminar. In fact, "a strong sense of shared purposes" is the ultimate environmental characteristic necessary for effective implementation of student-centered practices (Chickering & Gamson, 1987, p. 6), such as a first-year seminar.

In other words, as institutions consider the following information in the pathway toward providing leadership for a first-year seminar, it is appropriate that educators keep these in mind:

» Who are we as a college or university?
» What are we *not* going to be or do as an educational institution? In other words, what are the elements that we are comfortable letting go of with respect to our institutional identity?
» What is our aspirational state of being (i.e., vision)?
» What is our institutional mission? How is this communicated to members of the campus community and external constituents?
» What are the short-term and long-range strategies that will help us achieve our mission?
» What are our explicit and implicit commitments to students?
» Do our environmental structures and artifacts support the institutional mission and cultural values?

The answers to these questions can help identify institutional culture, examine how explicit and implicit messages support or contradict these values, and guide decision making about launching and administering a first-year seminar as well as other educational initiatives.

Once an institution has reviewed student data to determine student needs, gone through the process of understanding its institutional culture, and conducted an audit of its challenges and resources in support of a seminar, then the selection of the type of first-year seminar is a much more manageable task. In fact, when viewed as a part of this equation, the seminar becomes the medium to achieve course outcomes that effectively address student needs within the context of the institutional culture. The remainder of this volume will serve as an introduction to the process of adding elements to this equation that will result in successful implementation, administration, and refinement of a first-year seminar.

Chapter 2
Launching a Seminar

Many campuses have implemented first-year seminars to support new students in meeting the intellectual and social challenges of higher education. In addition to these student goals, there are often institutional expectations that the seminar respond to college access concerns unique to first-generation and/or low-income students while improving retention and graduation rates for all students Cavote & Kopera-Frye, 2004; Friedman & Marsh, 2009; Henscheid, 2004). The decision to launch a seminar immediately raises a number of questions for the campus, many of which may seem daunting. For example, organizers must decide how the seminar will fit into current services and efforts focused on first-year students. Other questions may include: Who needs to be part of the discussion related to planning and launching the seminar? and What steps should be taken to maximize the benefits for the students, faculty, and the campus community?

This chapter presents recommendations for launching a pilot for the seminar over the course of a 12-month period. The suggestions emphasize securing broad-based campus input during the development and administration of the pilot. While the initial offering may not be perfect, such broad-based support increases the likelihood of long-term program backing. Further, the pilot is essential for understanding the potential effectiveness of the seminar and for making improvements as the program is more widely adopted. Table 2.1 outlines steps that serve all institutions when launching a campuswide effort. The remainder of the chapter describes each step in the implementation process and the role of members of the leadership team in greater detail.

Initial Planning for the Pilot

The first -year experience is a campuswide responsibility, and a first-year seminar is a curricular response for exploring that experience. The decision to implement a seminar can be the work of one or the effort of a group. While

Table 2.1

Recommended Implementation Timeline for First-Year Seminar Pilot

Implementation timeline	Tasks
Month 1	Meet with provost or chancellor to identify leadership team
	Send letters of appointment
	Hold initial meeting outlining the task
	Engage in institutional audit
	Review campus mission and align seminar goals with mission
	Identify and assign members to action areas, including
	» curriculum development
	» administration and logistics
	» campus communication
	» instructor recruitment and development
	» student recruitment
	» seminar assessment
Months 2-3	Create a campus webpage that is updated regularly with names and contact information of leadership team members (communication team)
	Deliver charge to the leadership team (provost/chancellor)
	Make recommendations for seminar implementation (administration and logistics, curriculum development, and seminar assessment teams)
Month 4	Review and approve recommendations from curriculum development, administration and logistics, communications, and seminar assessment teams
Months 5-6	Identify instructor recruitment and development team that will
	» work with potential instructors
	» research faculty development models
	» recommend a preparation framework for instructor involved in pilot
	Identify student recruitment team that will
	» ensure students enroll in the pilot
	» determine communication concerns that would need to be addressed for broader implementation of the seminar

Implementation timeline	Tasks
Months 7-11	Teach pilot section(s) of the seminar
	Meet with instructors and students for midterm check-in (leadership team)
	Provide support to seminar instructors as needed (instructor recruitment and development team)
	Initiate seminar assessment to include
	» establishing baseline information for the program
	» developing and administering course evaluation
	» gathering other data (e.g., GPA, retention rates) for student assessment
Month 12	Evaluate pilot (seminar assessment team)
	» Meet with instructors to debrief
	» Review student course evaluations
	» Recommend program modifications
	» Update webpage with revised seminar information

the heroic energy of a single person seldom leads to a sustainable course or program, that may be the only starting point available on some campuses (Boyce, 2003). Yet, a broad-based leadership team will create the greatest level of expertise and knowledge for developing and implementing this course. Whatever the origin of the seminar movement on the campus, ideally, appointment to the leadership team will occur at the level of the chancellor, the provost or chief academic officer, dean, or similarly high-ranking administrator. This same administrator should be present at the initial meeting to provide the charge for the group and set the timeframe for project completion. After the leadership team has been established, other initial steps include conducting an institutional audit and identifying work groups for planning and implementing the seminar.

Establishing the Leadership Team

Any number of individuals can serve as ambassadors for the effort; however, the leadership team should represent the major stakeholders on campus while keeping the team small enough to manage the early stages of the work (AAHE, ACPA, & NASPA, 1998; Mandel & Evans, 2003; Schroeder, 2003). Some campuses have appointed an academic administrator as the lead but a well-respected faculty member or student affairs professional could serve in this role. It is strongly advisable to include a direct student services professional such as someone from academic advising or residence life. These campus educators are specialists in student development theory and provide invaluable perspective to the creation of a first-year seminar. Students can bring a dose of reality to the conversation and are an excellent resource often overlooked even when initiating something on their behalf (Light, 2001). Additional members of the campus can collaborate with the leadership team to flesh out the work to be accomplished, but the leadership team should be tasked with decision making. Institutions that are able to work and partner effectively across divisional lines are most likely to establish high-quality experiences for students (Barefoot et al., 2005; Kezar, 2002; Schroeder, 1999; Schroeder, Minor, & Tarkow, 1999).

Once the leadership team has been established, the team should consider creating a website where regular updates can be posted as planning proceeds. This will allow the campus to familiarize itself with the new initiative at the very earliest time possible. The website might also serve as recruiting tool for those interested in becoming involved in the effort. Whether the course implementation is the result of a grassroots initiative on the part of faculty and/or student development professionals or an administrative fiat, an understanding of how to become involved will support a message of inclusivity and shared responsibility.

Conducting an Institutional Audit

The first responsibility the leadership team will address, once established, is to assess campus readiness (attitudes and resources) for implementation of the seminar through an institutional audit. McGhee (2003) outlines an internal institutional audit process that can be used as a precursor to implementation of a first-year seminar. Such an audit will uncover the procedures that ensure quality, integrity, and standards across the institution and influence the capacity of the campus to sponsor the seminar. Since the audit is managed by individuals on the campus rather than by an external organization, it requires a willingness to confront and possibly change practices that may derail the launch of the course. The audit both communicates the intention of starting the seminar and highlights the individuals on campus who are willing and able to support its intended outcomes.

Equally important, such an effort will provide insight into who or what will need additional attention or information so that the work will be done. For example, most admissions offices communicate frequently with prospective students until they are enrolled in classes. Engaging this office in the conversation about the seminar should facilitate a set of sequentially appropriate messages about the seminar to incoming students and help them make an informed decision about enrolling in the course. Faculty from a wide range of backgrounds often provide first-semester or first-year course advisement for new students. Tapping into the advisor training program will ensure students receive a consistent message about the course.

Among the topics to broach during an institutional audit are:

» What is the mission of the campus, and what role should this seminar play in fulfilling that promise?
» How does this course fit in to the overall approach to the first year of college on this campus?
» What is the capacity of this campus to prepare and communicate what it is doing?
» What curricular innovations have been adopted in the past?
» What is the administrative will for this effort?
» What is the instructor development process on this campus, and how can it be used to prepare for course design and delivery?
» Is the predominant pedagogy on the campus instructor-, student-, or content-centered? How does that influence the seminar?
» Do academic affairs and student affairs work together on the campus?
» Who else needs to be involved?

Similar to the self-study phase of a regional or departmental accreditation visit, an internal audit gives those charged with implementation an opportunity to identify the offices, people, and policies that are key players in the success of the project.

Establishing Other Work Groups for the Pilot

In addition to the institutional audit, one of the early tasks of the leadership team is to identify the major steps for launching a pilot and to establish work groups or teams to manage those aspects of the implementation. Figure 2.1 presents a suggested organizational chart for a seminar implementation. A detailed discussion of the responsibilities of each work unit follows.

Communication team. Institutions of higher education depend on informed dialogue and broad-based communication to launch and sustain new initiatives. Before developing a local campus plan, members of the leadership team should gather information about a variety of seminar models and the outcomes associated with these models. The communication team is the group responsible for sharing this information with the rest of the campus. Once this

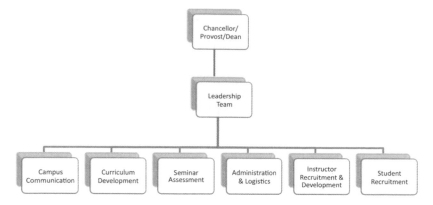

Figure 2.1. Suggested organizational structure for first-year seminar pilot.

team is established, it should make an effort to post new information about the seminar on a monthly (if not more frequent) basis. Suggested resources and information to be shared are included in Appendix A. Other information can be gathered through participation in listservs and electronic discussion groups and attendance at regional and national conferences. Gathering and reviewing resources is an important step in implementing a seminar. First, it provides a common knowledge base and language for the individuals who are involved in planning. Second, it creates an awareness of the number campuses and individuals who are already engaged in this work and increases the resources that can be used. Third, it provides educators with an awareness of where and how individuals and institutions can make a contribution to a fundamental aspect of higher education. Fourth, it takes what can feel like isolated and lonely work and turns it into the work of a community of learners.

Curriculum development team. This team researches the possibilities for presenting the seminar, prioritizes models, and makes recommendations for how the curriculum can be written. Additionally, the group ensures that a full range of curricular and cocurricular opportunities are considered. Requests and recommendations for course content and experiences should be elicited from both student and academic affairs colleagues. Ideally, the seminar will stress opportunities for greater student-faculty engagement, which may include undergraduate research, service-learning, global learning experiences (e.g., study abroad or cultural immersion), and community engagement. Such experiences may also be more pedagogically effective, as they stress the student's role in the process of knowledge creation rather than mere knowledge consumption.

Once the curriculum development team has developed a set of topics and issues associated with first-year seminars, the team needs to communicate curricular recommendations to the seminar assessment team. The development and use of a solid course assessment tool will allow instructors to identify specific curricular components that support students and the course objectives. Additionally, the curriculum development team should sponsor a set of campus-based conversations during the third or fourth month of the implementation timeline to introduce the course and the topics. Two to three sessions, presenting the same information, should be scheduled on different days and times and open to all members of the campus community. A special effort should be made to invite any individuals who have already indicated an interest in teaching the course. These sessions serve as a strong communication tool for the campus community as well as an orientation to the course for the faculty.

It is important to understand the campus culture when embarking on such efforts. For example, which individuals need to be involved to give the process credibility? Where is the most appropriate campus location to hold the information sessions? An excellent way to indicate the seminar's front-burner status is to have the chancellor, president, or chief academic officer announce the sessions and attend each of them in order to express enthusiasm for the work. The physical space for the workshop series will also influence the way it is perceived. If a dedicated and attractive instructor development space is not available, information sessions might be scheduled in the chancellor's boardroom, the CAO's conference room, or other similarly formal meeting space.

While the primary reason for the session is to broaden the campus knowledge base about the purpose of the seminar, the session will also assist in identifying faculty and staff who will support or undermine the effort. There is room for everyone who shows interest—supporters will assist in creating buy-in and skeptics will keep the process honest. The seminar needs to reflect the academic community in which it resides, meaning that everyone can have a hand in its creation. For example, supporters can be invited to plan the programming while skeptics are asked to assist with the evaluation process. To facilitate later recruitment of instructors, names of all attendees should be shared with the instructor recruitment and development team.

In working on the course content and delivery, the curriculum development team may recommend a set of guidelines for instructors to use when selecting books and readings for first-year students or the use of a common textbook to support course goals. The campus culture and type of seminar the campus hopes to offer will drive this recommendation and likely be made early in the process. If the seminar type suggests that instructors will select course materials individually, the committee should ask for assistance from a department familiar with the typical abilities of the campus' first-year students (i.e., English, Communication) to provide guidelines on selecting texts. Engaging faculty from those departments in workshops on how to teach first-year students would also be useful.

Should the seminar type lend itself to a common textbook, multiple options are available and more are published each year. Publisher representatives attend regional and national conferences focused on the first-year seminar and are more than willing to share desk copies with potential adopters. Additionally, authors often participate in conferences and meet with instructors to discuss their perspective on the seminar. Committees should take the time to map course objectives to multiple textbooks; the closer the match between course goals and textbook content, the more likely instructors and students will use it. There are many bells and whistles associated with text publishing, particularly regarding online content, and the curriculum development team should be realistic about whether an ancillary product is necessary to achieve the course goals. If instructors and students seek online support and materials, then these materials may prove invaluable. Providing training for how to use the textbook in the context of the curriculum will likely improve the willingness of instructors to engage students with the selected book. Given the rising costs of texts, it is important to students and parents for required texts to be utilized in the course. The first-year seminar leadership should avoid selecting a book, requiring students to purchase it, and leaving it up to the instructors to decide whether or not to use it.

Seminar assessment team. The seminar assessment team needs to work closely with the curriculum development and administrative and logistics teams to provide guidance regarding the development of course and programmatic outcomes. The primary responsibility of this group is to identify the indicators of success that meet campus standards and recommend assessment instruments or processes that will be used to gather evidence of progress in meeting those standards. Assessment of the seminar is a dynamic topic that is addressed more fully at a later point in this book and in the final volume of this series. Thus, only a brief introduction to the topic is provided as it supports efforts to identify an assessment team.

At a minimum, seminar assessment efforts should focus on student progress, instructor effectiveness, and program efficacy. For each area, it is useful to identify summative tools that guide judgments about the seminar and formative tools that support continual improvement. Most campuses routinely gather summative data; and rather than request the use of a new tool, it is wise to review what is already used and attempt to fill in the gaps. Institutional researchers (IR) in both the academic and student affairs areas can assist with this aspect of assessment planning. For example, a number of commercially available instruments, such as the College Student Expectations Questionnaire (CSXQ), College Student Experiences Questionnaire (CSEQ), Student Satisfaction Inventory (SSI), College Student Inventory (CSI), Your First College Year (YFCY), and National Survey of Student Engagement (NSSE), are commonly used on campuses. Staff in the IR office can help the assessment team identify relevant information being collected by such instruments and incorporate it into a larger assessment plan. Additionally, individuals who have expertise in formative assessment processes should be asked to assist with this committee. Faculty development specialists are excellent resources for this aspect of the work.

Administration and logistics team. This team works with individuals from the registrar's office, admissions, orientation, academic advising, and faculty senate or other governance body to determine any deadlines and/or processes that must be followed in implementing the pilot. New courses are often subject to college communication processes and approvals that regularly extend over several months. To the extent that new programs and pilot projects adhere to normal campus procedures, policies, and timelines, they are more likely to garner long-term support. For example, being aware of and adhering to the course publication schedule for the registrar's office is extremely important if the seminar is to be implemented on time.

Additionally, the administration and logistics team will recommend how the seminar should be funded and work closely with the campus administration to determine its capacity and will to implement the course. Many administrators will grant latitude to an idea or program, especially if it has the potential to assist them in responding to a matter for which they are responsible. More often than not, they need results that allow them to make budgetary decisions in a timeframe that seems at odds with the generative and developmental nature of implementing a curriculum. A frank conversation about timelines and measures can provide the urgency needed to keep the campus engaged and informed about the evidence of progress needed to proceed.

Once administrative permission is secured, it is important for key administrators to provide support. In addition to fiscal and physical resources, support means constant advocacy and awareness of what is occurring. Yet, different administrators need different information to be effective in their sphere of influence. Deans and chairs must justify their budget requests internally while presidents and chancellors often request funds externally. The administration team can work with the assessment team to begin the process of collecting data and stories to share with the administrators who are working on behalf of implementation of the seminar. In the early stages, the data can be as simple as the number of faculty and staff attending information sessions and what participants are saying about the possibility of starting a new class. Later on, the data should provide information about how students who take the seminar are meeting broader campus goals (e.g., selecting a major, participating in service-learning efforts, engaging in leadership experiences).

Instructor recruitment and development team. Relationships matter when the time comes to recruit instructors. Deans, department chairs, and faculty leaders are necessary assets for identifying instructors who are best able to meet the course outcomes. Involving these individuals in the task of identifying who should teach the course has the additional benefit of broadening the campus conversation about the seminar. Students are also able to identify faculty members who are both challenging and student-centered in their approach to teaching. Lists of teaching award recipients can be another source of faculty who are engaged in the classroom and who may be potential champions or instructors for the course. Finally, a campuswide call to all individuals interested in teaching the seminar should be crafted and distributed. To ensure a broad and diverse instructional pool, individuals from the aforementioned groups can be asked to serve on the instructor recruitment team. Because faculty in education or psychology departments often have pedagogical expertise or may have an increased understanding of the developmental needs of first-year students, representatives from these fields should be invited to provide leadership for faculty development.

While there needs to be a sense of inclusion in generating interest in teaching the course, it is equally important to be selective in recruiting the instructors who will work with the pilot effort. The instructors who are associated with the seminar will create its reputation. Colleagues who are proven early adopters or comfortable taking risks are logical choices for instructors of pilot sections. Similarly, those individuals who are concerned about the needs of first-year students and supportive of the program goals should be invited to teach. The first-year seminar must not be the dumping ground for faculty who are unsuccessful in their home departments. Once the course has a few years under its belt and has found success in meeting course objectives and serving students, it might be appropriate to invite faculty who are struggling in other areas to participate in the instructor development activities associated with the seminar. Improved teaching is a likely outcome of intentional faculty development, and the campus is likely to see benefits for seminar instruction and for other courses taught by participants (Fidler et al., 1999).

A preliminary application that explains the seminar, its proposed outcomes, deadlines for applying, and expectations for participation needs to be designed and widely available through the seminar website, as an attachment to e-mails, in departmental offices, faculty development center, and the library. Collecting pertinent contact details from interested faculty will allow the instructor recruitment and development team to pull these individuals together for informational and training sessions. It may also be useful to ask faculty and staff members to request a department chair signature on the teaching application. This requirement serves a two-fold purpose: it (a) broadens the campus conversation about the course and (b) reinforces the importance of working within the normal procedures of the campus by making chairs aware of possible obligations and interests faculty and staff in their departments have.

Informing the campus of the first-year seminar effort is different from preparing instructors to teach the course. The first effort is fundamental to the success of the initiative, but the instructor development component is crucial to the effectiveness of the seminar as a place of learning for students. A combination of readings, attendance at conferences, and campus-based preparation is an ideal instructor development program but is not always realistic.

If there is a campus center for faculty development or teaching improvement, a strong partnership is essential for developing this course. These individuals have knowledge of communicating with the campus regarding workshops and meetings. On some campuses, they have support staff and funds for traveling to conferences, bringing in outside consultants or speakers, purchasing publications, and/or reproducing materials. Additionally, meeting space, video conferencing capabilities, evaluation instruments, and campus-based consultation are often available.

Some campuses are too small or financially unable to centralize and fund a dedicated faculty and/or staff development program. Multiple alternative avenues should be considered if this is the case. For example, the campus library may be an excellent partner for this work as college librarians can assist the team in researching appropriate publications, films, and online and print resources.

Once the foundational knowledge has been gained, the instructor recruitment and development team will need to create an ongoing faculty development plan, which will be at the heart of the implementation process. First-year students are more likely to connect to and continue their educational experience on a campus when they know they fit in and belong; the same is true for the instructors. Convincing instructors to commit to the seminar and assist with improving it over a period of time requires that a supportive community be established to meet the challenges of teaching a course outside a home discipline. Without a person or team of people who can respond to questions and concerns of the course faculty, instructors will not commit to working on the curricular problems for the long haul.

Strategies for building an instructional community around the seminar include asking experienced instructors to mentor new ones individually or in professional learning community settings. Attendance at conferences—regional or national—allows instructors to understand national trends and concerns regarding the efforts of first-year seminar work on various campuses and helps integrate them into a larger educational community focused on first-year student learning and success. Additionally, setting the expectation that instructors present or publish their experiences reinforces the academic nature of the seminar and the responsibility to facilitate the learning of others (Fidler et al., 1999; Hunter & Skipper, 1999).

Models for faculty development are more fully explained in chapter 3 of this volume; however, as much as possible, faculty development for the seminar should mirror the pedagogical expectations of the course. If the seminar is student-centered, then the faculty development should be as well. Specific teaching techniques that encourage discussion and promote reflection need to be experienced by instructors in the context of preparation. For example, most faculty members do not dwell on personal issues when teaching a course in traditional academic disciplines. Yet, personal development is frequently a focus of first-year seminars. As students begin to connect with and trust teachers and classmates, it is common for disclosure to occur. Preparing instructors to deal with the responsibility of this connection to their students is vital to the success of the course (Braxton et al., 2000; Donahue, 2004; Hoffman, Richmond, Morrow, & Salomone, 2002-2003). It is not necessary for every instructor to present every idea or respond to all students in the same fashion, but it is important to provide instructors with a variety of strategies for successfully teaching the seminar.

Student recruitment team. Instructor enthusiasm for teaching a new course needs to be supported by informed students who enroll in the course. Enrollment does not happen just because the seminar is offered. The student recruitment team is responsible for coordinating all marketing and enrollment efforts. It is important to determine how the target population will be identified and when they will learn about the course. If all students are required to take the course, the seminar information should be presented during all admissions visits, reinforced on campus websites, discussed throughout summer orientation, and in all communication about the campus curriculum. If the seminar is being developed for a select group of students, then a more targeted invitation can be used to reach these students. An example of this would be a seminar designed to support first-generation students. Not all students entering the campus would qualify for such a seminar and, thus, an effort to identify first-generation students through appropriate sources is vital. In this case, if the campus supported one of the federal TRIO programs, such as Student Support Services, Upward Bound, Talent Search, or Educational Opportunity Center, then personnel from those programs should be involved in marketing the program. Because staff in these programs have well-established ties to students from first-generation backgrounds, they help send the message to the appropriate audience. Widespread knowledge about the seminar among campus personnel from admissions to orientation and academic advising is essential if the right students are going to register for it.

Implementing and Evaluating the Pilot

Once instructors have been selected and trained and students enrolled, pilot sections of the seminar will be taught. Clearly, a critical moment in the implementation of a new course is to evaluate its effectiveness, celebrate successes, and identify areas for future growth and improvement. Each team involved in the pilot needs to summarize their work, accomplishments, and recommendations for improvement. Establishing a ritual of celebration is a thoughtful way to support individuals who have committed time and energy to the effort. A breakfast or luncheon where the contributions of instructors and team members are acknowledged is one strategy for celebrating the success of the pilot. Photographs, student presentations, and short video clips posted to a website or shared during formal celebrations similarly acknowledge the work of those involved while sparking new enthusiasm for the seminar.

The communication team, in concert with the leadership team, should prepare a progress report for distribution to key administrators. Additionally, the communication team should update the website with pictures, student and instructor quotes about their experience in the seminar, and short statements about success. Information about personal experiences with the seminar strengthens recruitment materials and gives the campus a place to refer interested individuals to as they discuss the program. The seminar assessment team can begin the process of making meaning out of the data collected and the evidence produced around the course outcomes. The student recruitment and instructor recruitment and development teams must review their processes and update their messages to better reflect the seminar experience. The administrative and logistics team needs to review its effectiveness in meeting deadlines and supporting the seminar for the pilot offering and, if increased offerings are in the making, modify processes and make recommendations for its work.

Creating Campus Buy-in for Student Success

Obtaining a critical mass of support for the first-year seminar will help the campus move toward what Gladwell (2000) calls the *tipping point* and Collins (2001) refers to as the *flywheel concept*. In other words, systemic change comes after slow, painstaking work over long periods of time and through the hands of many people. Typically, change only becomes noticeable to a large number of people after the really hard work has been done. It is not uncommon for first-year experience proponents to report years of experimentation before the seminar or other first-year efforts surface as an important element in the campus culture. It is through the intentional linking together of a range of efforts—recruitment, admissions, orientation, advising, residence life, out-of-class engagement, learning assistance, and the first-year seminar—that students will most benefit from a campus-based first-year experience. It is this comprehensive approach, one that crosses budgetary and supervisory divisions, that truly brings the campus together for learning.

The work of first-year student success belongs to many individuals and offices on any campus. It is simply too important to be done alone. Every campus has resources that support students and faculty, but few campuses truly embrace sharing these resources for universal concerns. Collaboration is a different way of working for most faculty and administrators and yet, it can be the most rewarding way to establish a campuswide community of learners. The key to campus buy-in is allowing all of the parties the opportunity to see their own work in the creation of the project's goals and vision. In doing so, connections are made, understanding is fostered, commitment is forthcoming, and project goals are advanced. The end result is that students have access to the greatest number of resources because they are coordinated and combined on behalf of their success. Some of the typical areas of connection for sharing this work include common reading programs, campus orientation, leadership development, admissions offices, writing centers, library orientations, learning assistance centers, residence halls, student engagement efforts, learning communities, academic advising, service-learning, general education, and living/learning initiatives.

Among the most crucial partnerships to be fostered on behalf of student success is one between academic and student affairs. The Boyer Center at Messiah College (Grantham, PA) initiated an assessment, supported by the Fund for the Improvement of Postsecondary Education (FIPSE), of such efforts from 2001-2005 and identified seven principals of good practice for such partnerships. Ideally, they (a) reflect and advance institutional mission; (b) embody and foster a learning-oriented ethos; (c) build on and encourage relationships; (d) recognize, understand, and attend to institutional culture; (e) depend upon specific partnership outcomes and ongoing assessment; (f) use resources creatively and effectively; and (g) demand and cultivate multiple manifestations of leadership (Whitt et al., 2008). The end result is to create what Kuh, Kinzie, Schuh, Whitt, and Associates (2005) call the seamless learning environment, which connects purposes, processes, and practices with student needs and abilities in the context of shared learning. Application of knowledge out of the classroom is evidence of learning inside of it. The ultimate goal is for students and educators to engage in learning and improve the overall institution.

A first-year seminar is only one of the multiple tools a campus can employ to ensure that students and faculty actively engage in meaningful work. It is not a silver bullet that will solve rocky financial foundations, student dissatisfaction with parking, or faculty frustration with administration. It is, however, a microcosm of the campus that can reveal the truism, whatever is happening with our students is also happening with our faculty and staff. If students are disengaged on campus, then it is a sure bet that faculty and staff are as well. A well-designed and adequately supported first-year seminar demands intentional engagement by the entire campus community. Furthermore, it should be a relevant contributor to the student abilities and learning outcomes expected by faculty in subsequent years as well as a formative experience that students refer to in evaluations about their college experience.

Chapter 3
Administering the Seminar

So often, it can take herculean efforts to get the interest and support to start a first-year seminar. Once institutional leaders have determined the need and solicited the support necessary to begin this venture on campus, they are then faced with the difficult task of administering a meaningful and sustainable course. In many ways, this is where the heavy lifting comes in. For example, the decision to offer a seminar or to revamp and refine an existing one is immediately followed by many, if not all or more, of the following questions:

» What are the appropriate learning outcomes for students who participate in the seminar?
» Where will the administration and oversight of this seminar reside in the organizational structure?
» How will the course be funded?
» Which seminar type is the best fit for the institution? Will more than one type of seminar be offered?
» How much credit should the seminar carry and what kind?
» Which students will take the course?
» Who should serve as course instructors?
» How will we recruit and train seminar instructors?
» What pedagogical practices should instructors use in the course?
» How will achievement of seminar learning outcomes be measured?
» How will program effectiveness with respect to the course be assessed?

This chapter will address many of these questions as well as follow upon the steps to developing and launching a first-year seminar (chapter 2) with an emphasis on the ongoing maintenance and delivery of the course. First, the topic of learning outcomes linked to seminar purpose and goals is addressed. Drawing upon this foundation, the section is followed by a thorough discussion of course leadership, administrative location, and budgetary issues for first-year seminars. The next section covers the myriad decisions that are inherent in the organizational structure of the course including the number of contact hours, course size, offering the course as a requirement, and the connection of the seminar to other institutional initiatives to form an integrated and comprehensive first-year experience. Given the importance of instructors to the achievement of the learning outcomes for first-year seminars, the chapter builds on the overview of instructor recruitment and training offered in chapter 2 and provides notes on pedagogical approach in these courses. The chapter concludes with a brief introduction to the components of an assessment program for first-year seminars that ensures that the courses are progressing toward their stated goals. In sum, this coverage is intended to provide a flexible outline and points of consideration for administering different types of first-year seminars in a variety of institutional contexts.

Learning Outcomes

It may seem strange to some individuals to begin a discussion of course administration with the desired end point. However, a journey without a destination likely leads to aimless wandering. Similarly, without identifying the desired outcomes of administering a first-year seminar, the course is likely to lack curricular cohesiveness and impact. While this process should begin during the development and launch of the course, most notably through the work of the seminar assessment team as discussed in chapter 2, successful first-year seminar administration is contingent upon ongoing consideration of relevant, current, and meaningful learning outcomes. Therefore, a key question to ask in the administration of a first-year seminar is, What will we be able to show that students have learned or gained as the result of their participation in this course? (Gahagan, Dingfelder, & Pei, 2010).

Too often the discussion of desired outcomes of a first-year seminar is limited to the issue of retention. In fact, retention is a common reason for launching a new seminar and, thus, a frequently used measure of effectiveness (Griffin & Romm, 2008; Hunter & Linder, 2005; Padgett & Keup, in press; Tobolowsky & Associates, 2008; Tobolowsky et al., 2005). However, even if first-to-second-year persistence is the reason of greatest political and practical importance for a first-year seminar on a given campus, it is valuable to broaden the scope of outcomes for the course beyond this single variable. First-year seminars have the potential to have a positive impact on the retention rates of new students, but they often do so indirectly via other levers. The first-year experience is a complex, integrated, and multivariate experience that is inclusive of curricular and cocurricular experiences; personal, interpersonal, and academic development; and myriad interpersonal relationships. Any of these experiences, skills, and relationships—either alone or in combination—could be the predictor(s) of students' decision to return to college for the second term of their first year or as a sophomore the following year and, thus, are valuable outcome measures in and of themselves.

The most commonly used correlates of retention include student satisfaction and grade point average, which are often easy to measure via student surveys and readily available institutional data. However, identifying outcomes of first-year seminars should be inclusive of other critical components of the new student experience and guided by student needs. Are first-year students leaving the institution because they feel disconnected from or dissatisfied with it? Then perhaps creating a common new student experience, orientating students to campus resources and services, and developing a support network among peers should be important course objectives. Are new students struggling academically or in their major? If so, developing study skills, enhancing cognitive complexity, or introducing students to a discipline may be valuable learning outcomes. If they are leaving because they feel personally lost, identity development and values clarification would be important outcomes for the seminar. Further, when everything that is happening in the lives of new students is coupled with the time spent in a course, especially a high-touch class like a first-year seminar, there is the potential to affect many aspects of students' lives and, accordingly, a high likelihood that a first-year seminar should identify and address multiple outcomes. Table 3.1 identifies many examples of first-year seminar outcomes in various categories. However, this is in no way a comprehensive list, and each institution should strive to identify first-year seminar learning outcomes that fit their student needs and campus culture.

First-year seminar outcomes must also be student-centered in their developmental appropriateness. Many of the skills that educators try to instill in new students during their first year are ones that they will continue to address and refine throughout their educational career and their lives. It is important to set high expectations for students but also to embed any learning outcome within the developmental context of the particular student population and the duration of the seminar. For instance, if a campus suffers from balkanization along racial or ethnic lines or a lack of student diversity, multicultural competence may be a desired outcome of its first-year seminar. However, it may not be realistic

Table 3.1
Sample Learning Outcomes for the First-Year Seminar

Domain	Learning outcome
Retention	Persistence to the second year
	Graduation rates
Academic skills/experiences	Analytical and critical thinking skills
	Development of educational career goals
	Declaring a major
	Knowledge integration and application
	Academic engagement
	Academic achievement
	Cognitive complexity
	Study skills
	Introduction to a discipline
Campus connection	Knowledge of university requirements
	Ability to identify, seek, and use organizational resources and student programs
	Feeling connected to the campus community
	Understanding institutional history and traditions
	Involvement in cocurricular activities
	Satisfaction with the student experience
Interpersonal skills	Conflict resolution
	Written and oral communication skills
	Development of a social support network
	Multicultural competence
Personal development	Time management
	Identity exploration and development
	Values clarification
	Practical competence
	Life management skills
	Physical health
	Emotional wellness
	Moral and ethical development
	Leadership skills

Domain	Learning outcome
Civic engagement/democratic citizenship	Participation in service
	Engagement in philanthropy
	Political awareness/engagement
	Community involvement
	Involvement in political activism/social advocacy

to expect that adolescents in their late teens or early 20s will fully achieve this personal goal in a single semester. As such, a more appropriate outcome of the first-year seminar may be to advance their understanding of their own cultural identity as well as to introduce a framework and vocabulary for intercultural discussion and exploration. In another example, getting students to engage in meaningful debate and dialogue in class and in writing assignments often takes the development of cognitive complexity. It may take an entire term just to get students to recognize and question their previous academic habits and dichotomous ways of thinking and to identify the skills to see multiple sides to an argument or a host of possible answers to a question, let alone fully incorporate conceptual complexity into their academic practices.

One tactic to help identify important developmental thresholds for outcomes of first-year seminars is to identify and use a developmental theory appropriate to the outcome of interest. For example, the steps included in King and Baxter Magolda's (2005) Developmental Model of Intercultural Maturity could help provide a framework for meaningful seminar outcomes related to multicultural competence while King and Kitchener's (1994) Reflective Judgment Model provides guidance related to promoting cognitive complexity. Similar to other stage theories,[2] these models have established thresholds of development that can help formulate an appropriate outcome statement for a first-year seminar, identify meaningful measures of progress, and suggest what it will look like when students in that course have achieved the desired outcome.

---

[2] Stage theories describe how humans, particularly as children but also in their development of maturity as adults, move through a pattern of distinct stages over time. These stages are organized in a hierarchical fashion (i.e., an individual must complete a lower stage to progress to a higher plane of development) and can be described based on their distinguishing characteristics. Thus, rather than gradually changing in an unorganized manner, humans typically shift to different plateaus of perception and behavior in an orderly and predictable fashion (Evans, Forney, & Guido-DiBrito, 1998; Pascarella & Terenzini, 1991, 2005)

Another valuable resource for the identification of meaningful learning outcomes are sets of standards offered by disciplines, student affairs associations, or accrediting bodies. In the past several decades, higher education has experienced the dawn of an accountability movement, which has led to a great deal of self-study in this field and the burgeoning of a host of processes, instruments, and criteria to gauge educational effectiveness and development. Perhaps the most notable of these processes are from the Council for the Advancement of Standards (CAS) in Higher Education, which offers a general set of desired outcomes for the undergraduate experience as well as specific self-study guides for areas of the university that are intended to provide support for students and a framework for assessing learning and developmental outcomes. While CAS guidelines and resources are generally focused on student affairs, similar standards, benchmarks, and criteria addressing the academic experiences of students and learning in the cocurriculum have emerged from a number of sources. These include accreditation bodies; the Association of American Colleges and Universities (AAC&U); the disciplinary associations that guide the activities of departments, majors, and faculty; the Foundations of Excellence in the First College Year* from the John N. Gardner Institute for Excellence in Undergraduate Education; and the sponsoring organizations of national survey instruments, such as the National Survey of Student Engagement (NSSE), the Cooperative Institutional Research Program (CIRP), and Educational Benchmarking, Inc. (EBI). While such an array of choices can further complicate a difficult process of identifying the appropriate developmental goals for new students, they do provide a number of frameworks for selecting, measuring, and achieving meaningful outcomes of the first-year seminar. No longer must educators begin from scratch in this process. Instead, these resources provide a host of off-the-shelf options for identifying and measuring learning outcomes. However, more often than not, these resources provide a starting point for consideration or a template rather than a wholesale solution and must be adapted to fit the student needs and institutional culture to ensure seminar success.

Course Leadership and Administrative Home

As outlined in chapter 2, there is usually an implementation committee responsible for exploring, developing, and launching the first-year seminar. Typically, this committee is inclusive of a variety of individuals from across the campus such as faculty, academic administrators, student affairs professionals and students, and has the support of departmental, divisional, college, or institutional leadership. Further, this committee is often comprised of several teams whose members have specialized skills and specific goals in the development of the seminar, including a communication team, curriculum development team, seminar assessment team, and recruitment teams for both faculty and students. In these teams, members of the implementation committee serve a number of different roles including stakeholders, ambassadors, content experts for course development, and champions for seminar adoption.

One of the critical points in the life cycle of a course is the transition of leadership for the first-year seminar from this implementation committee to the administration team that will provide ongoing oversight for the course. In most instances, the administrative team includes several of the members of the implementation committee and, in the best scenario, other members of the planning teams will remain involved as important advocates for the seminar in the campus community and/or as instructors for the course as shown in Figure 3.1. However, the individuals who are able to gain the momentum to begin the course on campus are not always the same people who are best positioned to maintain this momentum, oversee the delivery of the course, provide the seminar an administrative home, and move it from new initiative to institutionalized campus offering.

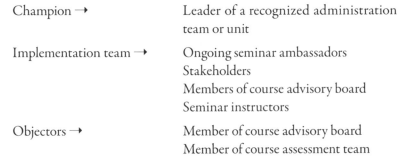

Figure 3.1. Transition of roles from implementation to administration.

It is particularly important to transition to an administration team when the early efforts are associated with one champion of the first-year seminar implementation. In the early phases of the course, it is an incredible asset to have one person on campus who provides the face and leadership for course consideration and implementation, especially if that person is a well-respected and well-liked member of the campus community. However, at a certain point in the adoption of the course, an ongoing association with one person on campus can make the course vulnerable as it is identified as someone's pet project or unsustainable if the early champion is reassigned to another campus unit, adopts another institutional change effort, or leaves the institution altogether. Creating shared course leadership across a number of positions and formalizing its administration as a part of the professional duties of a number of individuals will build a stronger foundation for the seminar and contribute to its organizational sustainability.

If it is acknowledged that someone or, even better, a team of colleagues needs to take on the mantle of ongoing leadership, the question then becomes, Who should do so and where is the best administrative home for the first-year seminar? National data show that first-year seminars more often reside on the academic side of the institution under academic affairs generally or with a college or school (e.g., College of Liberal Arts, College of Education), academic department, or in a university college (Tobolowsky & Associates, 2008). Further, programs that have a director or dean of the first-year seminar tend to draw the person for that leadership role from the faculty or academic affairs. Being structurally associated with the academic activities of the institution can have some significant benefits, such as greater involvement from faculty, perception of greater academic rigor, the increased likelihood of course credit counting toward general education or the major, the opportunity for seminar leadership to be included in important discussions about campus curriculum and teaching, and budget allocation from student tuition and fees. Given their purposes as outlined in chapter 1, first-year seminars that are academic, either with uniform or variable content, and preprofessional seminars may find that being housed in an academic unit or under academic affairs is a particularly good fit.

Although the majority of first-year seminars have an administrative home in academic affairs, a significant minority is housed in a different unit on campus. For example, approximately 13 to 14% of first-year seminars are administered by student affairs (Padgett & Keup, in press; Tobolowsky & Associates, 2008). Others find an administrative home in residential life and housing or enrollment management, and a growing number are in first-year or new student program offices. While seminars that are housed in these areas run the risk of being perceived as tangential to the core academic mission, they also have several benefits. Student affairs personnel and other institutional staff, for example, are often overlooked in the teaching pool for seminars administered by academic affairs or departments. However, as the number of administrators and staff on a given campus often outnumbers the number of faculty members significantly, the pool of instructors for courses administered from student affairs and other nonacademic units is broadened significantly. Further, these courses often pull from outside the academic realm to address a broader range of new students' educational and adjustment experiences, including issues that are the foundation of the cocurriculum and personal development. Given the wide range of topics and broader purpose of extended orientation first-year seminars, an administrative home in student affairs or housing may be a more meaningful fit than oversight from academic administration.

While one can weigh the pros and cons of having a first-year seminar administered from academic or student affairs, the truth of the matter is that successful first-year seminars are more frequently the result of effective collaboration between these two sides of the house, regardless of where course administration is situated within the organizational structure. New student experiences span a wide domain of educational opportunities both inside and outside the classroom. As such, first-year seminars are likely to have learning outcomes that are academic, personal, social, and interpersonal. Further, the demand for economy requires avoiding duplication within the academy, which is much more likely if efforts are claimed by only one unit in the organization. Effective and efficient educational practices to achieve outcomes of first-year seminars will need to draw upon the expertise and support of multiple colleagues across the campus and not remain entrenched in a particular discipline or domain of the university. Historically, higher education has operated in vertical silos; however, structures such as first-year seminars are more horizontal in nature, drawing from multiple domains of the university and cutting across historic boundaries to collaborate in the process of supporting students in their transition into and through the university (Keeling, Underhile, & Wall, 2007). Therefore, regardless of where the seminar is housed, it is important to include campus partners from across the institution in the course administration either by involvement in course development and review, teaching, communication and public relations, assessment, or in an advisory capacity. Further, it is important that the administration team, advisory board, and any formal advocates for the course are acknowledged publicly in these roles. The inclusion of their names in biographical sketches on the seminar administration website and providing them with an official title for their involvement in the seminar to complement any other roles that they have on campus will be important to creating institutional buy-in and leadership for the course.

Funding and Budgetary Issues

Another element of first-year seminar administration that is intimately coupled with course leadership and administration is the matter of funding the course. While this is an aspect that will likely come up during the initial consideration and development of the seminar, it is important that it receives ongoing attention. Typically, course funding strategies are dependent upon where the course is situated in the organizational structure and the budget model for the institution at large. Courses that have an administrative home on the academic side are more frequently funded with a proportion of student fees or allocation of budgets through colleges, departments, or majors. Seminars administered through student affairs will more frequently receive funding through allocations from a centralized division or department of student affairs. Those administered by residential life or enrollment management may draw from auxiliary funds, such as revenues generated from admissions or housing fees.

Although many funding questions will be pre-empted by these institutional structures, a number of the same elements comprise the budget for these courses, including (a) central staff and office support, (b) seminar instruction, and (c) instructional support.

Central staff and office support. Salary and other support for course leadership and administration will be an item in the course budget. While some first-year seminars are administered as a portion of a professional position or as an overload and others are managed by an entire department of staff, a base cost of any initiative includes salary, benefits, fringe, professional memberships, and professional development funds for staff.

In addition to the *who*, a seminar program budget has to consider the *where* from an administrative perspective and account for facility costs for the central staff as well as supplies, technology, and other support for effective operation of these facilities and the staff therein.

Seminar instruction. Certainly, instructor compensation will be a significant cost associated with the seminar budget. However, it also represents an expense that is often highly structured by campus personnel policies and compensation guidelines and, potentially, by state mandates for public institutions. While monetary compensation is certainly the most familiar remuneration to most individuals, it is important to consider all types of compensation, including course release time; graduate student support; professional development funds; and, in the case of student instructors, tuition remission or course credit, in order to manage the direct and indirect impact of compensation on the seminar budget.

Recruiting a pool of talented instructors and investing in their ongoing training on seminar content, pedagogy, and skills to support interaction with students is a significant expense in seminar administration but also a critical investment in the outcomes of a first-year seminar. As mentioned elsewhere in this volume and series, instructors are the most important aspect of first-year seminar success and, thus, their recruitment, initial training, and ongoing development should remain a core element of the course funding model.

Although instructors and teaching assistants are the primary teaching staff for a first-year seminar, it may also add value to involve guest lecturers, supplemental speakers, service-learning opportunities, or field trips to the curriculum for the course. Often, additional instructional staff is drawn from colleagues across campus, and the institutional calendar of events is the focus of classroom outings. However, paid speakers, performers, or off-campus events may provide unique educational opportunities that are worth a line item in the seminar budget.

Instructional support. Although many seminar models recoup the expense of course textbooks, guides, and other instructional materials, a course budget needs to be able to extend the funds to support the purchase of these materials before the seminar coffers are replenished by the funds collected from their sale. Further expenses may be incurred if first-year seminar programs choose to develop their own textbook or materials, want to underwrite the cost of such materials for first-year students, or provide copies or teachers' editions of these materials to the instructors.

As students become savvier with information technology, more courses, including first-year seminars, are incorporating online components and other computer-based technologies into the curriculum. While some of these technological advancements may be downloaded for free from the Internet or represent part of general IT support from the university (e.g., course management systems, instructor websites, online tutorials in basic skills), there has been a significant increase in the number of educational technology resources available for purchase to support student success initiatives. Over the past decade, higher education has witnessed a virtual cottage industry emerge of student support products ranging from game-oriented software to address financial literacy or healthy living to online modules to assess knowledge of substance use and abuse to customizable social networking media. While many of these products represent valuable tools to enhance the education experiences of first-year students and achieve seminar learning outcomes, they must also be accounted for in the budget for the course. Additionally, any training expenses to ensure seminar staff, instructors, and students have facility with the technology must also be considered.

While the dawn of technology has certainly moved society closer to a virtual world, it is difficult to conduct day-to-day instructional operations in academe in a paperless work environment. Therefore, while it is easy to overlook the mundane expenses of copying and office supplies, they represent an important component of effective teaching and learning.

Even with these general categories, the development and maintenance of a budget can feel overwhelming, especially for those with little or limited experience managing accounts. However, there are several general guidelines to keep in mind with respect to budgetary oversight of a course that can both assist in general management and introduce new ideas and sources of revenue for the seminar:

» Much like the transition of leadership, the transition of funding needs to be addressed in the life cycle of a course. New initiatives can be started with an infusion of institutional funds or a grant, but it is critical to sustainability that recurring funds be identified for ongoing course support.

» A fundamental component of budget development and management is understanding the nature of one-time expenses versus recurring funds. One-time expenses, as their name suggests, are seminar costs that are a one-shot investment in the course that have a long shelf life and utility for the seminar. Examples include (a) the purchase of a new course management system, (b) acquisition of resources and materials for an instructor training library, or (c) technological materials to supplement the course. Conversely, recurring expenses are base costs of the seminar budget that will reappear with each seminar cycle or fiscal year, such as seminar staff and instructor compensation and instructional support. While there may be economies over the years, recurring expenses will always represent a line in the seminar budget while true one-time expenses do not. It is critical to recognize that even expenses that appear to be one-time often require ongoing investments, although perhaps not on an annual basis (e.g., a new software package will eventually need to be updated with a more current version). It is important to categorize seminar expenses appropriately and ensure that the seminar has enough ongoing financial support for the recurring expenses to sustain the program.

» Since the first-year experience is typically a horizontal structure in higher education, involvement of multiple units on campus may introduce a number of different streams of support for the course. Further, student success initiatives (e.g., first-year seminars) often have numerous stakeholders outside the institution, such as alumni, parent/family organizations, contributors to institutional foundations, community partners, and entities that serve as common employers of graduates. Both internal and external constituents may provide a source of core or supplemental funding for the course. Therefore, it is valuable to think as expansively as possible when considering partnerships and resource opportunities for a first-year seminar.

» It is important to realize that seminar support can take multiple forms in addition to funding, including human resources, class space, instructional staff, training opportunities, among others. A thorough review of all possible resources as well as acknowledgement of nonmonetary contributions will be of benefit to course administration and sustainability.

» When economies are gained from effective collaboration across campus, it is possible that those savings can be directed to the core budget of a course.

» In order to prove return on the investment of funds for the administration of the first-year seminar, assessment and funding must go hand in hand. It is important that the course not only have clear learning outcomes but also that it has an assessment plan to document a baseline before course implementation, progress toward learning outcomes, and evidence that this progression can be linked to the course. Further, it is critical that any assessment activity include a plan for the dissemination of findings to the campus community, institutional leadership, and seminar stakeholders.

» When administering a course, it is critical to keep course scope and goals within the budgetary parameters. Nothing will undermine the notion of return on investment and create the appearance of poor stewardship of resources more than an overextended course structure and administration budget. It is better for long-range success to start small and grow steadily than it is to create a large-scale, but ultimately unsustainable, seminar program.

Resources and sound fiscal management are critical to any educational initiative, including first-year seminars, and can often become the primary focus and concern of seminar leadership. However, emphasis on the budget should never overtake an emphasis on the students in the administration of these courses. Funding and budgets are important vehicles to advance the developmental goals and educational outcomes of first-year seminars, but resources do not in and of themselves guarantee success. Many first-year seminar programs are highly effective with very few funds while numerous highly resourced programs have not been sustained. Funding is but one variable, albeit an important one, in a multifaceted equation for seminar success.

Seminar Structure

When deciding the structural elements of the course, it is important to return to a student-centered model of education. A host of theories in higher education extol the benefits of student involvement in the classroom and in the cocurriculum including Pace's (1984) Quality of Student Effort, Astin's (1984) Theory of Involvement, Kuh and associates' (1991, 2005) assertions that engagement is a key factor to effective educational practice, and Chickering and Gamson's (1987) "Seven Principles of Good Practice in Undergraduate Education." All decisions about the way the course is structured and delivered—regardless of which type of seminar, where it is housed, and who represents the leadership—should focus on enhancing the engagement of students in the learning experience.

Contact Hours and Credit

To ensure that the students are having the opportunity and encouragement to engage fully in learning, the number of contact hours is a significant consideration in the structure of a first-year seminar. Further, since most faculty and administrators still abide by the adage that students should spend two to three hours outside of class focused on course material for every one hour in class and since credit hours are the measure of in-class time, it is important to consider whether the first-year seminar should be a one-, two-, or three-credit course. First-year seminars that bear three or more credits afford the greatest opportunity for coverage of course content; the establishment of appropriate conditions and expectations for student involvement; and the development and maintenance of students' relationships with faculty, peers, and campus staff. Further, first-year seminars that bear the same credit as other courses toward general education or one's major are far less likely to be seen as ancillary to the academic mission of the institution. Courses that bear less credit run the risk of being seen as a curricular addendum, potentially undermining the perceived educational value of the first-year seminar. Buy-in may be further enhanced when these credits count toward graduation in fulfillment of general education requirements or in the major, although national data show that many first-year seminars are offered as an elective without credit toward general education or the major (Padgett & Keup, in press; Tobolowsky & Associates, 2008).

Since many colleges and universities are limited by institutional policy or politics from administering a three-unit first-year seminar, it is important to note that institutions should not look at number of credit hours as an all-or-nothing option with respect to the three-credit course model. Research has shown that courses with fewer credit hours can be effective at achieving a limited range of learning outcomes (Swing, 2002). For example, a one-credit course "is as effective as courses that meet for more hours per week" if the course goal is to introduce students to campus resources, policies, and practices (Swing, p. 1). Two-unit courses are far less frequent than their one-hour or three-credit counterparts, most likely because they do not fit typical models in higher education of a standard course or a one-unit special section course, but they do provide the opportunity to address a few more outcomes or plunge into greater depth on a single course objective than one-credit courses. While it is important to be aware of their limitations, having a one- and two-unit seminar is much better than none at all and can help students make progress toward a carefully considered set of learning outcomes. Further, the establishment and administration of such a course makes a significant statement about the value of new students to the campus community and the desire to support them during their transition into and through the university.

Course Size

In addition to course credit, course size represents an important lever for engaged learning in first-year seminar. At its core, the purpose of a seminar is to create a smaller, more engaged learning environment where students can plumb greater depths with respect to the course content. Historically, these smaller, intense courses in which depth is prioritized over breadth have been the hallmark of upper-division classes and often represent capstone experiences in a major or discipline. However, first-year seminars have been one of the primary vehicles to provide these same benefits of smaller classes to new students. Much like courses with greater contact hours, smaller classes create the conditions under which students will respond to high expectations for participation and increase the opportunity for interaction among peers and between the students and instructional staff. This increased interaction is likely to forge relationships that will serve as an academic, and potentially social and personal, support structure for first-year students. However, smaller class size and the expectation of increased participation also allows professors and students to engage in small-group discussion and debate, role-playing methods, case study exercises, and write-to-learn exercises—teaching techniques that are often not possible in larger classes (Erickson, Peters, & Strommer, 2006; Erickson & Strommer, 1991; Light, 2001). Not only do these techniques require a smaller number of students for the instructor to manage these processes, but they also often require the trust and community that can only be built in smaller course environments.

In response to this understanding of the benefits of smaller classes, educators often ask for the magic number for seminar enrollment in order to maximize the educational experience. In many respects this debate has been addressed by the research on class size, but the answer provided by college ratings systems has been the one that has created the most significant message about course size. Most notably, *U.S. News and World Report* uses the measure of courses with fewer than 20 students as a gauge of academic quality in their rankings system, thereby creating a national benchmark for seminar size. Although many institutions still strive to meet this threshold, several colleges and universities, particularly larger institutions, fall short of the goal to have seminars with fewer than 20 students. While the implications of this situation upon rankings should be fully considered, it is important not to become discouraged if a class size under 20 is not feasible. It is still valuable to provide first-year students with classes that are small enough to provide meaningful and engaged learning and the opportunity for interpersonal interaction and support. For some colleges, first-year seminars may be fewer than 10 students while other institutions may need to include 20-25 students to be able to manage the course administratively and otherwise, which may still represent a significantly smaller class experience than other lecture-hall style lower-division classes.

Requirement Versus Elective

Another element of first-year seminars to consider is whether to administer the course as a curricular requirement or structure it as an elective. In some ways, other considerations indicate the appropriate choice for this decision. For example, how widespread are the student needs identified in the campus audit? If they are fairly uniform across all segments of the new student population, then it may make sense to address them with a required first-year seminar. Further, how the credit for the course is applied may suggest whether it is wise to require the seminar of all first-year students or not; credit that is applied toward graduation as part of the general education requirements is much more conducive to a universal requirement than are seminars that are more major specific in their credit allocation. Similarly, the type of seminar selected may also impact the required versus elective decision. Most notably, extended orientation courses and academic seminars may be more realistic to require of all new students while preprofessional or discipline-linked courses and basic study skills may not be.

While these factors provide some direction about whether the course should be required or elective, there is no fixed formula; and other issues are likely to enter the discussion about this decision. The most notable of these issues is related to the resources that are necessary to administer a first-year seminar to the entire new student population at an institution. Expanding the scope of the program to cover everyone also immediately increases the scope of resources and infrastructure needed to make it successful (e.g., instructors, classroom space, faculty training) with very little option of leveraging any economies of scale. Therefore, one runs the risk of diminishing the overall quality of the program if expanding its reach to include all students goes beyond the scope of its funding, staffing, and other resource models. Further, requiring students to participate can foster a negative impression of the seminar, creating a deficit for instructors to overcome in their efforts to achieve course outcomes. Conversely, by leaving the decision regarding participation to the students, it is entirely possible that the very students who need the course will choose not to take it and that enrollment will merely represent the decision of high-performing students who, although they may gain from the course content, are least in need of its assistance.

One option that effectively blends the benefits of both required and elective models while diminishing the negative impact of each is to use the information gained from an ongoing process of student data collection and interpretation as well as from the institutional audit to identify populations that are in particular need of transition assistance and require the first-year seminar of that sample of students. One way that institutions are identifying these targeted student populations in need of first-year seminars is to craft formulas of expected persistence and academic performance based upon the success factors suggested by national assessment agencies (Astin & Oseguera, 2005; NSSE, 2009; Pryor et al., 2009) and proven with institutional-level student data. Similar analyses are being conducted on other outcomes generally and on students in the disciplines, especially majors with high failure or emigration rates, to help identify particularly problematic areas of students' transitions. This type of pre-assessment allows first-year seminar leadership to be more targeted in issuing requirements for the course to students who may be at particular risk in that college environment while also allowing other students to elect to enroll. Some populations that may be required to take first-year seminars include provisionally admitted students, undeclared students, student athletes, and students in specific majors. Further, not all students who are required to take a course represent at-risk populations, and some may even be in premier programs that can benefit from a seminar structure, such as honors students or undergraduate research fellows. In any event, targeting requirements toward specific populations allows the course to reach the desired students and avoid undermining buy-in and overextending resources.

Connection to an Integrated First-Year Experience

Finally, the decisions made about the structure of a course should also include a connection to other existing curricular and cocurricular programs intended to support new students. Too often, educators confuse a first-year seminar with a first-year experience (FYE). While these seminars may be the cornerstone of the first college year, in and of themselves, they do not meet the general standards of an FYE program. More specifically, Barefoot et al. (2005) suggest that institutional excellence in the first year is characterized by an "intentional and comprehensive approach to improving the first year," which includes a variety of initiatives (pp. 6-7). Where possible, the administration of the first-year seminar should include intentional linkages to other campus programs, such as (a) orientation and welcome week activities, (b) learning communities, (c) service-learning, (d) academic advising, and (e) peer leadership and mentoring.

Orientation and welcome week activities. These programs introduce the ethos of campus culture; the expectations for student success at the institution; and the campus resources, faculty, administrators, and peers available to support that success. Since these elements are also often the foundation of successful first-year seminars, orientation programs and welcome week activities represent perfect partner programs to such courses.

Learning communities. Barefoot (2002) indicates that learning communities include a single cohort of students who enroll in two or more linked courses across the curriculum. National research reveals that learning communities are being used by nearly two thirds of four-year institutions across the country, most frequently in large research extensive universities, and are often used with first-year students (Barefoot, 2002). Although first-year seminars and learning communities can be integrated in various ways, Henscheid (2004) collapsed the number of roles that first-year seminars play in learning communities "into two metacategories: one in which the integration of learning across the learning community experiences creates primacy, and the other which foregrounds community building" (p. 2).

Service-learning. Zlotkowski (2005) describes service-learning as "a course-based service experience that produces the best outcome when meaningful service activities are related to course material through reflection activities" (p. 358). Service-learning is a perfect example of a more involved teaching technique that can be effectively used in a small class, such as a first-year seminar, and conversely, the first-year seminar is the ideal environment to conduct the kind of thoughtful reflection needed for the success of service-learning initiatives.

Academic advising is a critical element of academic success in the first year, but it is often ineffectively or underused by new students. By connecting advising with the first-year seminar through class activities or by using advisors as seminar instructors, students are more likely to make effective use of advising services.

Peer leadership and mentoring. In most campus environments, there are numerous opportunities for first-year students to be the recipient of peer leadership and mentoring, including advising; orientation; residence life; Supplemental Instruction; and counseling for physical, emotional, and personal health care needs. First-year seminars provide an opportunity to introduce new students to these important peer resources as well as provide a platform for one of the fastest growing areas of peer involvement: teaching (Keup & Mullins, 2010). National data indicate consistent, albeit low, use of undergraduates as peer leaders or co-instructors of first-year seminars (Padgett & Keup, in press; Tobolowsky & Associates, 2008). Given the increasing use of peer educators in other academic domains, such as advising, Supplemental Instruction, and tutoring, and the educational and economic benefits of using peers as leaders, mentors, and teachers, it is likely that the use of peer instruction in first-year seminars will increase in the future (Keup & Mullins).

While not a comprehensive list, these programs offer examples of other building blocks to complement first-year seminars in a meaningful overall first-year experience. In the most successful scenarios, such programs are used in combination and in connection to create a constellation of educational opportunities and support services for new students (Barefoot et al., 2005; Upcraft, Gardner, Barefoot, & Associates, 2005).

Instruction and Pedagogy

In almost any classroom scenario, the instructor is the most influential and important factor for success, and research shows that "learning outcomes and student satisfaction with first-year seminars are highly correlated with the way teachers conduct first-year seminars" (Swing, 2002, p. 1). Further, unlike a class in a particular discipline where poor pedagogy can hide behind content mastery, the content and outcomes of first-year seminars are often process-oriented and require strong teaching to facilitate that process and shepherd the student toward the desired outcomes. Finally, as mentioned previously, one of the major strengths of these seminars is that they are smaller in size and, thus, allow the instructor to use more innovative and engaging teaching techniques compared to other lower-division courses. Swing was able to empirically identify teaching components and classroom practices that were highly correlated with positive outcomes of the seminar, such as critical thinking and students' perceptions of overall course effectiveness. Together, these practices were called engaging pedagogies, and their hallmarks include (a) a variety of teaching methods, (b) meaningful discussion and homework, (c) challenging assignments, (d) productive use of class time, and (e) encouragement of students to speak in class and work together.

Engaging pedagogies represent guidelines for practice rather than a prescription for teaching, which allow for their application to different types of first-year seminars; variations in course content; as well as different instructional styles, strengths, and approaches.

Instructor Recruitment

Recruitment is the first step in the process of ensuring an effective instructor pool. While most seminar administrators will be inclined and conditioned to engage members of the implementation team and mine faculty colleagues to teach first-year seminars, these are far from the only sources of good instruction on campus. Student affairs colleagues represent another highly knowledgeable pool of teaching professionals as do academic affairs administrators. In fact, if the seminar is administered out of either of these units on campus, it makes a strong statement of buy-in and ownership to draw instructors from the ranks of administrative staff in those areas. Additionally, inviting instructors from the highest ranks of the institutional structure, such as the president, provost, and vice-presidents, communicates investment from campus leadership. Even if a first-year student is not in the section with the president or provost, it is an important statement that those campus personnel are willing to invest their limited time teaching first-year students.

Advisors represent another valuable pool of potential teachers. When these colleagues are paired with first-year advisees in sections, it can represent a particularly powerful learning experience. Inviting the leadership and personnel from the other first-year experience programs, such as orientation, service-learning, residential life, Supplemental Instruction, and learning communities, is a way to strengthen the ties between programs in an integrated first-year experience and expand the instructor pool. Over the past 10 years, registration for national conferences on FYE issues and participation in the national dialogue on student transitions via publications and listservs have reflected an increased investment in and advocacy for first-year students among campus professionals not historically or uniquely associated with first-year students, such as librarians, career counselors, mental health care professionals, and staff from disability services. These colleagues often make excellent instructors or guest lecturers for first-year seminars and are uniquely qualified to address certain course topics (e.g., information literacy, selection of majors and identification of career paths, stress and emotional well-being, and inclusivity, respectively) or particular subpopulations of first-year students. Finally, given their vast experience with the institution and ongoing commitment to its success, there have been more recent movements to engage both alumni and emeritus professors to teach first-year seminars.

One other valuable resource for instructors is the student body themselves. Institutions with graduate programs, particularly doctoral programs, have a large pool of individuals who are pursuing a pathway to the professoriate and may welcome an opportunity to teach undergraduates. Additionally, there has been a growing interest in higher education in engaging upper-division undergraduates in an instructional capacity as peer educators. In its truest form, peer education provides an educationally purposeful activity for both the educator and the recipient with significant benefits to both parties. First-year seminars provide a wonderful platform for upper-division peers to provide instructional support and personal mentorship to new students. While engaging peers in the seminar may introduce challenges from an employment and compensation perspective, fellow students represent a plentiful, potentially economical, and mutually beneficial option for program administrators.

Instructor Training

Training represents the second step in the process of ensuring an effective instructor pool. Given the importance of the instructor's role in the course, instructor training is critical to the success of the seminar and should be a large portion of the operating budget for any first-year seminar program. Whatever initial preparation is provided, a plan for ongoing support and development should also be considered. As noted in chapter 2, this might include mentoring by experienced instructors, attendance at regional or national conferences, and the expectation that instructors present or publish on their teaching experiences. Engagement in ongoing instructor training and support is critical to the early success and long-term sustainability of a seminar, so program leaders should be upfront about their expectations when recruiting instructors and realistic about the rewards implemented to encourage their ongoing participation.

The same models for instructor development and support that were introduced in chapter 2 as part of launching a seminar are also excellent opportunities for faculty training throughout the lifespan of the course. Participation in national conferences; the development and support of campus workshops and institutional conferences; and investment in a library of reference materials and scholarly publications for seminar instructors on first-year students, adjustment issues, and teaching and learning are all useful tools to support both new and returning seminar instructors. Other examples of instructor training draw inspiration from the structure of various educational initiatives for first-year students themselves. These include a semester-long series of workshops (similar to a course), new instructor orientation events, mentorship of new instructors by more experienced ones (modeling peer education), and the creation of faculty learning communities. As such, the impact of first-year seminars and other curricular interventions has also expanded to the education of faculty and staff on issues of teaching, learning, and pedagogy.

Assessment

As mentioned previously, assessment should be infused throughout the process of planning, developing, and launching a first-year seminar. For this volume, we will use the definition of assessment offered by Palomba and Banta (1999) in which they state that assessment is a formalized collection, review, and use of information about educational programs for the improvement of student learning and development. Assessment will be a valuable component of the institutional audit performed during the process of developing and launching the seminar as discussed in chapter 2. Assessment information gathered prior to course implementation will serve as the baseline against which to judge the need and impact of the course, while student data gathered from ongoing assessment activities will serve as a guiding force in the decisions made during course administration. Because improvement of educational programs is an ongoing process, assessment must be as well.

Given the iterative nature of program assessment and improvement, it is helpful to use one of the many models for this activity to guide its practice. The one adopted for this book series is a multiphase assessment cycle by Maki (2004), which includes identifying outcomes, gathering evidence, interpreting evidence, and implementing programmatic change based upon the interpretation of evidence. Given these changes, the cycle would begin anew with the identification of outcomes based upon the programmatic change and so on.

Since the identification of outcomes is an aspect of course development, implementation, and administration, and thus has already been addressed, we will begin with the step related to gathering evidence. An understandable first assumption about this stage of assessment is that one must go out and gather new information, which can be a costly, time-consuming, and, if assessment expertise is thin among first-year seminar staff, somewhat intimidating prospect. However, an important aspect of gathering evidence is the process of documenting what is already known and the data sources that are currently available. Too often, the decentralized nature of higher education institutions leads to the manic collection of data with very little interpretation and utilization. As such, campuses may have a virtual gold mine of information in the form of admissions data, registrar's data, administration of national survey instruments for first-year students, utilization statistics, reports generated by the institutional research office, accreditation reports, student satisfaction surveys, and course evaluations to name just a few potential sources. These existing data can provide valuable insight into the needs and expectations of new students; salient outcomes for first-year seminars; the new student populations in greatest need of this curricular intervention; content to include in the course; key characteristics of students who do or do not take the course; and the development, satisfaction, and learning of students in the course.

Once an understanding of currently available data has been established and what it reveals about first-year students fully explored, there are a number of different decisions that guide the process of gathering new information to measure progress toward seminar learning outcomes, including

» The selection of a framework for data collection that addresses whether there will be a comparison group for the assessment and who or what will serve as the point of comparison, such as:
  • Criterion-referenced assessment in which the program or students are compared to a set of predetermined standards of performance or development
  • National benchmarking in which progress and achievement of outcomes is compared to students or programs at a similar institution (i.e., peer referenced) or at institutions that represent an aspirant comparison group
  • Trends analyses in which students are compared to previous cohorts at the same institution
  • A value-added approach that measures a student's change over time in development, performance, or outcome (most frequently with a pre-/posttest design)
» Use of formative assessment practices (i.e., "using the process of gathering evidence to facilitate improvement," Bauer, 2003, p. 11) or summative assessment, which is collecting data and information "for an external reason such as program continuance," approval, or accreditation (Bauer, p. 11)
» The ability or practicality of measuring the outcome of interest directly, as with grade point average or retention, or employing a proxy measure of performance or development (i.e., indirect measures), as with the development of leadership or multicultural competence
» Selection of primarily statistical methods, narrative, or observational inquiry or the decision to draw from both (i.e., a quantitative, qualitative, or mixed-methods approach)
» Use of a national survey instrument, such as those offered through the Cooperative Institutional Research Program (CIRP); Noel-Levitz; Educational Benchmarking, Inc.; the National Survey of Student Engagement (NSSE); or a locally developed, institution-specific assessment tool

One important caveat when making these decisions is that none of them represent choices with mutually exclusive options; it is completely acceptable and sometimes advisable to engage in more than one option for each decision. Although there are resource limitations to consider, all assessment data will inform course development, progress, and success. While these questions and choices may seem overwhelming, there are many higher education and first-year seminar assessment resources available to help inform this process, several of which are outlined in Appendix B. Further, all of these decisions should be connected to and informed by the learning outcomes that have been identified for the seminar. Thus, the purpose and goals of the seminar will drive many of the decisions around the assessment of the outcomes.

The audit of previously collected data and process of collecting new data is sure to reveal interesting findings, but it is important to spend time with these assessment results and identify their significance to the first-year seminar. In other words, it is important to answer the So What? question and address the real meaning and value of assessment findings. What conclusions can be drawn from the data? What new questions do the findings raise? What are the implications for practice, and how might the findings influence decisions? It may be valuable to include other colleagues in this process of interpreting findings, such as course instructors, the seminar advisory committee, members of the various implementation teams, a group of former first-year seminar students, seminar stakeholders, and members of institutional leadership. It may even be a useful exercise to include some of the strongest objectors to the course to hear an alternate take on initial interpretations of the data. Involvement of these groups can add viewpoints, create more holistic thinking, generate dialogue around the course, be a tool for creating buy-in for the seminar, and help disseminate the findings. Again, the learning outcomes for the seminar should serve as a touchstone throughout this process.

The final stage of assessment is to actually implement change based upon the interpretation of findings. Part of this process is sharing the interpretation of findings with a wide array of colleagues and stakeholders for the course to help implement any necessary change. The intended outcome of assessment is to continue effective practice or initiate change and improvement based upon assessment results and implications. One of the most challenging aspects of this process is discontinuing something that is not working. It is easy to become attached to certain practices or approaches within the seminar and continue them long beyond the point of relevance. However, the process of assessment allows the campus to constantly challenge its assumptions about what is working and what needs improvement by delving into the empirical evidence. In order to reap the benefits from an investment in assessment, it is important that everyone involved trusts the process and findings and act with integrity based upon them.

Conclusion

While not a formula for perfection or a silver bullet, these steps, questions, and considerations will help guide the administration of a first-year seminar. With any institutional initiative, there is a long journey from initial consideration, as discussed in chapter 1; to development and early implementation, which was addressed in chapter 2; to administration, as covered in the current chapter. However, every educational venture is an iterative activity that requires constant evaluation of the program to ensure long-range sustainability and success. The next chapter will address how to effectively create a process of reflection and refinement to ensure positive momentum for revamping and revitalizing the course, ensuring program sustainability, and maintaining success of the first-year seminar.

Chapter 4
Managing Change in the First-Year Seminar

All higher educational curricula are in constant flux; first-year seminars are no exception. Multiple reasons bring about change, even when an established first-year seminar has garnered awards and shown evidence of success. To remain relevant, a seminar must attempt to reflect the needs of the current student population, the state of campus resources, as well as the pedagogical agility and abilities of the instructors. Student success is not a traditional academic discipline, and thus it is a topic for continued faculty discussion and development, particularly as instructors retire and new ones join a campus. The campus curriculum reflects the experience, knowledge, and consensus of a community of individuals, whether it is driven by one or two outspoken individuals, a scholarly society, a campus department, or a whole institution. As a campus community's membership shifts, a first-year seminar might be tweaked, modified, abandoned, or revived.

Campuses change their first-year seminar most often because a perceived or proven course need, such as curricular rigor, effective program leadership, and/or student outcomes and behaviors, has not been addressed. Another influence that may lead to revisions of a first-year seminar curriculum is the predominant pedagogy of an institution's upper-division courses (Kain, 2003). If the first-year seminar creates an expectation for a different style of teaching and learning than is experienced in the upper-division courses, then the first-year seminar is likely to be out-of-alignment and possibly out-of-bounds in the eyes of upper-division students or faculty (Centra & Gaubatz, 2005). Additionally and more positively, the individuals leading the seminar become attracted to new ideas and models through reading the literature, participating in conferences, and engaging in conversations with multiple colleagues.

This chapter takes up the question of how a campus relaunches or redirects a first-year seminar, regardless of its history on a campus. As such, it will provide an overview of commonly noted drivers for change, a discussion about the difference between change and transition, and end with a set of suggestions for managing the transition associated with change. In doing so, the chapter will attempt to answers questions about the processes needed to support current and future efforts related to course purpose, administrative home, leadership, and the individuals who should be involved in these processes.

Drivers of Change

Assessment

A dynamic assessment process that connects student learning and course outcomes to the campus mission is among the strongest ways to both improve and sustain a seminar. Results from this type of process should allow course revisions and modifications to occur as a normal process without constant fear that the course will be cut. High-quality assessment tools and processes—homegrown or licensed—should be part of the support for the seminar. Instruments such as the National Survey of Student Engagement (NSSE) combined with institutional data (e.g., grade point averages, retention rates, major declaration rates, graduation rates) can provide a solid foundation for implementing change and refocusing a seminar that is not working or not working as well as it might particularly in light of the fiscal and human resources expended.

The assessment process should also be recursive, allowing the seminar to reflect new directions and concerns as the campus mission and priorities change. For example, if the percentage of students receiving financial aid and loan defaults is increasing, the institution may prioritize efforts to reduce the default rate. Course administrators may respond to this new perceived need by incorporating information on money management in the seminar or revising existing curricula on the topic. Longitudinal assessments of loan default rates for course participants can demonstrate the seminar's effectiveness in responding to changing institutional priorities and needs. Similarly, if an institution is unsuccessful in retaining out-of-state students, course administrators may choose to examine whether course practices can be modified to help these students connect to the institution. Finally, if the campus would like to redistribute the percentage of students declaring specific majors, course administrators may examine the seminar's effectiveness in introducing students to lesser-known majors.

Abilene Christian University (Abilene, TX; Tobolowsky et al., 2005) assessed its seminar's success with improving library skills using three different instructional models: (a) scavenger hunt, (b) simulated research, and (c) course-related research. An eight-year longitudinal study supplemented with comments from course instructors, student focus groups, and librarians found that library skills taught in the context of research, and particularly course-related research, was the most effective model to adopt. Data associated with all three models showed a positive influence on the development of library skills. However, the use of authentic assessment processes created an environment for a change in instruction from the scavenger hunt model to the more complex but more effective course-related research model (Tobolowsky et al., p. 11).

California State University, San Marcos studied the effect of its seminar on student continuation rates and academic success by comparing fall and spring semester data of students who took the course to those who did not. Demographics for both groups were similar. Students who took the course were more likely to continue and to have higher grades, leading to a recommendation to extend course offerings to all new students (Tobolowsky et al., 2005).

In both of these cases, information was purposefully gathered, interpreted, and shared. Determining which pedagogy was more effective for delivering a learning outcome was data-based and not reliant on intuition or instructor preference. The honest comparison provided a compelling case for adopting a particular curricular model at Abilene Christian University. The use of data at California State University, San Marcos illustrates the importance of paying attention to the quantifiable elements for monitoring the success of a first-year seminar (e.g., retention rates, grade point averages, time-to-degree, out-of-state vs. in-state enrollment). These measures do not share the entire story of the seminar, but they can be telling. In both of these examples, the argument for change was grounded in evidence. This has the advantage of making change a less divisive process and thus, more acceptable to a greater number of individuals.

Changes in Leadership

Assessment is an important tool for driving course change, but many changes are driven by persuasive personalities or new leadership. Even the dialogue associated with the search for new leaders can sometimes lead to the articulation of a new direction or, at the very least, a sharpened focused on what the campus has the capacity to deliver. Following the retirement of Appalachian State University's (Boone, NC) long-time provost and ardent supporter of Freshman Seminar, a new provost outlined his vision for general education reform. After two years of study, review of program assessment, campus forums, surveys, and focus groups, the General Education Task Force recommended a vertically aligned general education program that included a required, theme-based first-year seminar taught primarily by full-time, tenure-track faculty in classes no larger than 22 students. Faculty would receive multiyear appointments with credit hours in their home department and participation included in the departmental evaluation process (General Education Task Force, 2007).

The new seminar differed significantly in content, course pedagogy, and outcome measures from the previous seminar model that had been offered since 1987. An extended orientation course, the original seminar was designed to acquaint students with the opportunities and demands of higher education; support them in their transition to the university; foster cognitive and psychosocial development; broaden horizons; and assist in developing relationships with faculty, staff, and peers. Instructors were drawn from every area of the campus and often included appropriately credentialed community members (Tobolowsky et al., 2005). The new, faculty-taught seminar was designed to help students think creatively and critically and communicate effectively. The original seminar enjoyed a high elective enrollment of more than 60% of first-year students and received national recognition as a successful model (Barefoot et al., 2005). The move from this successful course model created both anxiety and excitement on campus.

Faculty members were enthusiastic about the development of an introductory course focused on a broad interdisciplinary question or topic. Further, the newly envisioned seminar reflected recently articulated goals to more fully ground the course in the general education curriculum to be required of all entering students in fall 2009. Still, abandoning a successful practice in favor of an unknown and unpracticed model is challenging for a campus community. Trust in new leaders and strong support from them must be evident for this level of change to succeed.

Campus Reorganization

Demands for efficiency, effectiveness, enhanced communication, and elimination of duplication lead many campuses to consider programmatic reorganization on a regular basis. Since the work of first-year seminars belongs to all, it is natural for it to become the nexus of multiple units. Important opportunities can be leveraged during reconfigurations as is illustrated in the 2006 reorganization at Harvard College (Cambridge, MA; Goodwin & Schuker, 2006). In an effort to address several areas in need of improvement, the College tied several first-year initiatives together in one area. These efforts included an expanded first-year seminar, a newly created office of advising, personnel support for social programming, and renovation of key areas in the library and first-year residences. The goal was to allow a team of individuals to come together to think about the student in a more holistic manner while meeting a need for increased student-faculty contact, improved academic advising, and greater social interaction. Similarly, Yale (New Haven, CT) sought to more fully integrate the efforts of the first-year seminar in its campus culture with the creation of the Yale College Seminar Office in 2009. By joining the first-year and residential college offices into a single entity, Yale combined its more recent innovation of a first-year seminar with its recognized tradition of a residential college seminar (Subrahmanyam, 2009). Through the reorganization of offices and realignment of personnel, campus leadership signaled a commitment to the course while providing additional support for long-term sustainability.

In some cases, reorganization creates anxiety and uncertainty for the individuals working in the affected units, which is most often the reason for resistance. As long as the focus remains on providing seamless support for the academic success of students, the changes should be invisible. Yet, it takes thoughtful, inclusive, and open communication and time to overcome the anxiety associated with resistance.

Economic Realities

It would be shortsighted not to mention the impact of economic downturns on first-year seminars. Despite the compelling arguments that well-designed first-year seminars improve first- to second-year retention and overall student persistence and increase student engagement, small seminars are seductive targets for cost savings. Because first-year seminars frequently belong to the whole campus rather than a single department, they may be particularly vulnerable to cuts. The itinerate nature of faculty who teach the course—on loan from an academic department, adjunct instructors, or staff members and all with allegiances elsewhere—further complicates the issue. Program administrators are usually the only voices of defense for the course, and they are easily drowned out in the cacophony surrounding financial survival.

During lean budget times, seminars may be eliminated altogether or be forced to make changes that undermine their effectiveness. Like many public institutions, the University of North Carolina (Durham, NC) faced severe budget shortfalls in fall 2009. In response, the University reduced course offerings and increased enrollment in existing sections, with seminar enrollments rising from 18 to 24 students per section. As one professor noted, "With 24, it's not a seminar anymore. Everything is sort of compromised" (Price & Ferreri, 2009). While administrators might legitimately suggest that there will be a minimal effect on student outcomes whether there are 20 or 24 students in course taught in an adequately resourced classroom by an engaging instructor, such changes may create dissatisfaction nonetheless.

Different Students, Different Needs

It is not unusual for campuses to provide or require participation in a first-year seminar for only a subset of students initially. In this way, seminar administrators learn how the course should be organized, and the instructors can be prepared to teach it without risking failure on a large scale. As success is achieved on a smaller scale, first-year seminar leadership may expand offerings and support different groups of students. East Carolina University (Greenville, NC), for example, revised its first-year seminar to serve groups of students who might otherwise not connect with campus resources or the broader campus community. Seeking to improve retention, the institution implemented a one-credit-hour first-year seminar open to all of its 3,600 entering students. Typically, more than one third of first-year students enrolled in the seminar. In 2006, the campus recognized a need to tailor some sections to meet the needs of specific populations on the campus, including first-generation students as well as off-campus and commuting students (Campbell, 2006). The willingness of campus leaders to acknowledge the many different types of students attracted to the institution as well as how they might encourage these students to support one another led to an important distinction among the seminar sections.

New Research and Curricular Innovation

Research is the lifeline of innovation on college campuses. Encouraging faculty and administrators to ask questions about their work, read about the experience of others, publish and/or present their experiences is fundamental to campus membership. To do something without documenting the results is a lost opportunity in higher education. If others cannot learn from what has been done, then it is as if it did not happen. Much curricular innovation during the past 20 years has occurred because of knowledge gained through general education reform that has developed or renewed a focus on information literacy, writing across the curriculum, learning communities, service-learning, undergraduate research, and diversity efforts. Examples abound of first-year seminars serving as a keystone for these efforts on campuses. In many cases, curricular innovation created significant changes in the delivery of the seminar, which, in turn, provided new directions for the general education curriculum.

The first-year students at the University of Rhode Island (Kingston, RI) benefitted directly from Gilchrist's (2007) research on information literacy. The library staff used student response data and Gilchrist's research on engaging students in both research and learning to revise the information literacy component in the seminar (MacDonald & Izenstark, 2008). Vanderbilt University's (Nashville, TN) College of Arts and Science new undergraduate curriculum (AXLE), approved for all fall 2005 entering students, combined its first-year seminar with its newly researched campus writing initiative and even changed the name of the course to First Year Writing Seminars. In doing so, the campus believed it could help students pursue their intellectual interests and provide them a solid introduction to the liberal arts (Sloop et al., 2004-2005). Service-learning has also influenced the critical thinking and writing skills of students. At College of William and Mary (Williamsburg, VA), faculty found that each year a small group of first-year students arrived who were proficient Spanish speakers but not analytical writers. To improve critical thinking and writing skills, service-learning was incorporated into a Spanish language first-year seminar experience, transforming a "bordered introductory writing course into a critical cultural studies course" (Arries, 1999, p. 41). Convinced of the importance of undergraduate research, the University of Illinois at Urbana-Champaign created the Discover Program in 1998 to provide first-year students with opportunities to enroll in small, faculty-led research seminars (Merkel, 2001).

The first-year seminar is an excellent curricular resource for both experimentation and integration of innovative efforts because it often values process rather than content. As such, it is infinitely malleable while simultaneously serving as an agent of change.

Change Versus Transition

Change is relatively easy—we simply stop doing one thing and start doing something else. Transition, on the other hand, is more complicated. It involves managing the emotions, thoughts, and questions that result from the decision to make a change. The transition process takes time and requires comprehension, integration, and possibly acceptance of the change.

Managing the Transition

Communicating a change or changes to an existing program is an important part of the transition process. A thoughtful communication plan will include a formal presentation to the campus administrative leadership (e.g., president's cabinet, dean, chairs, faculty council), but it will also include a range of other campus stakeholders. These stakeholders might include faculty, admissions representatives, academic advisors, orientation leaders, financial aid staff, and a host of other individuals who help students succeed in college. The communication plan should consider which messages need to be delivered to which stakeholders and at what times. Regular and timely updates about changes to the seminar allow the individuals leading the change to receive feedback and consider the impact of proposed changes on others. Such updates should help stakeholders understand why and how changes are being made. An active website can facilitate dissemination about proposed and ongoing changes. The greater the openness, the greater the campus engagement in the change will be. Good communication enhances collaboration and facilitates successful transitions.

Kotter (1995, 1996) offers other suggestions for managing transitions:

Build the guiding team. Having the right people in place with the right emotional commitment and the right mix of skills to guide the transition is critical. To facilitate the work of the transition team, seminar leaders should provide opportunities for team members to work together over time and in a variety of environments (e.g., meetings rooms, meals, on campus, away from campus).

Get the vision right. The team should establish a simple vision and strategy for communicating and managing the change. The clarity of the end point will allow the team to harness their emotional and creative resources for completing the work at hand.

Increase urgency. The team will guide the transition, but they must also inspire people to move by making objectives real and relevant. They can provide deadlines by which the proposed change or components of the larger work must be completed. Similarly, they should identify specific times for reports of progress in meeting objectives for both communication and accountability purposes.

Empower action. The team must help remove obstacles to change, provide constructive feedback and support, and celebrate progress and achievements.

Create short-term wins. One strategy for managing large-scale change is to set early objectives that are relatively easy to achieve so that individuals asked to adopt new systems or structures do not feel overwhelmed or discouraged. Identifying a manageable numbers of initiatives and finishing early stages before starting new ones will help those involved feel a sense of accomplishment and greater control of the process.

Do not let up. Because transition takes time, team leaders will need to encourage determination and persistence by highlighting what has already been achieved and reminding stakeholders of future milestones.

Create and invite change. While change for change's sake is not particularly useful, little is gained from being afraid to change or being so enamored of past successes that individuals do not feel it is necessary. Seminar leaders can reinforce the value of successful change via recruitment, promotion, and new leadership. Moreover, developing a record of successful transitions and presenting them to the campus can help the college or university embody the spirit of a learning institution.

There is no guarantee that using these processes will allow a campus to avoid stepping on the toes of individuals long associated with a previous iteration of the seminar, but it places the new leaders on firmer ground when recommending such changes. Problems will arise, including opposition from certain groups or the discovery that there is a lack of skills, knowledge, or resources. Given the time and focus, these elements can be corrected, change implemented, and transition to a new way of being can occur. Changing the curriculum inevitably brings change to the institution and requires intentional and careful management. Curriculum innovation reflects a proactive institution, one capable of adopting and supporting continuous improvement.

Chapter 5
Concluding Thoughts: Sustaining and Institutionalizing a First-Year Seminar

After launching a new educational initiative, such as a first-year seminar, and finding a formula for successful ongoing administration and refinement, it is often tempting to engage in the proverbial victory dance and feel as if the work is complete. However, despite the fact that higher education is often criticized for being notoriously slow to change, colleges, universities, systems, and even higher education writ large does, in fact, undergo transition and even transformation. Whether it is due to new institutional or program leadership, shifts in student populations or needs, emerging pedagogical approaches and teaching tools, identification of new learning outcomes or a host of other reasons, as identified in chapter 4, many things can happen in a campus environment with potential importance and impact for courses and curriculum. As such, all programs, including first-year seminars, are in need of ongoing attention; advocacy; oversight; and review to predict, recognize, and respond to these changes that ensure the sustainability and long-range success of the course.

The goal of this concluding chapter is to identify some important guidelines and themes to ensure ongoing effectiveness and excellence in the first-year seminar. This chapter will (a) identify elements from common student success models for first-year students that provide a foundation for the process of launching, administering, refining, and sustaining a seminar; (b) identify some general best practices that pave the way to continued success for the course; (c) begin to expand the perspective of the discussion of first-year seminars and contextualize them within a larger framework of initiatives for an integrated and comprehensive first-year experience and educational trajectory through college and beyond; and (d) close with a look ahead to the future volumes in this book series on first-year seminars.

Striving for Excellence in the First-Year Seminar

Freidman (2009) identifies relevance and excellence as the prescription for first-year seminar success. The key to relevance is ongoing attention to the content of the seminar in continual efforts to address the question, "Is the course doing the right things?" Course effectiveness is the hallmark of excellence, which corresponds to the question, "Is the seminar doing things right?" (Freidman). To ensure relevance and excellence, several models of student success in college emphasize the importance of environmental receptiveness to, and even a motivation to effect experimentation and improvement.

Kuh et al. (2005) identified an improvement-oriented ethos as one of six conditions that are critical to student success in their comprehensive, national study to document effective educational practices (DEEP), of which first-year seminars are an example. They found that highly effective educational environments "seem to be in a perpetual learning mode" to adapt and adopt programs that are consistent with "their priorities and commitment to student success" (p. 133). Institutions with successful programs are rarely deterred by resource limitations or structural barriers. Rather, they embody a sense of positive restlessness that continues throughout the life of the educational initiatives and translates into ongoing advocacy; positive evaluation; relevance; excellence; and ultimately, program sustainability.

Similarly, Barefoot et al. (2005) identified "a culture that encourages idea generation...and experimentation" as a hallmark of institutional excellence (p. 383). In an examination of best practices and successful environments for the first-year experience at 13 model institutions across the country, Barefoot and colleagues (2005) found that cultures that sustained and supported ongoing efforts toward positive change, akin to those practices identified by Kuh and Associates (2005), were those environments that allowed innovation, such as a new first-year seminar, to become an integrated component of a comprehensive student support program on campus. Further, such a cultural commitment toward experimentation and innovation allows those involved in a first-year seminar, whether the course is brand new or decades old, to embrace new ideas, pedagogies, and approaches as well as take collective ownership for the innovation. With the constant evaluation of the way things are currently done and receptiveness to new ideas, a first-year seminar is sure to make significant progress toward relevance and an ongoing pursuit of excellence.

While a programmatic and institutional ethos of innovation is a foundational element of maintaining relevance and excellence for first-year seminars, there are a number of other guidelines for best practice toward seminar sustainability and success:

» Formalized review is a valuable tool for more comprehensive evaluation of the relevance and excellence of the first-year seminar. It is certainly possible that a course may have a more formalized program of review embedded in its development and administration. If so, the steps of the formal review would likely mirror the stages of launching a new program as identified in chapter 2 or draw from existing self-study programs, such as the Foundations of Excellence® process sponsored by the John N. Gardner Institute for Excellence in Undergraduate Education or the self-study guides developed by the Council for the Advancement of Standards in Higher Education. Whichever process is selected for this review, it is important that the review team include historic critics of the course and new voices as well as ongoing advocates to ensure a balanced and informative review process. Further, it is also valuable to align it with institutional or programmatic cycles of review, accreditation, or evaluation and to engage institutional leadership in the process.

» While a formal review is a highly valuable exercise, it can also be very labor and time intensive, making it more suitable as a regular but infrequent process. Therefore, the first-year seminar must also allow for an ongoing process of authentic assessment, which provides a broader basis for understanding what students actually know and can use from what they are being taught. Responses are not based on predetermined options but rather illustrate or demonstrate the application of information in a variety of contexts. Portfolios, projects, presentations, and practicum or field experiences are examples of educational activities that have the potential to reveal a student's learning process. When students and faculty engage in authentic assessment, basic skills are evident but more importantly, higher level, critical thinking is revealed.

» Education is indeed about change, and curriculum needs to be current but it is also important to pay homage to the historic players and processes that helped pave the way for current first-year seminar success. Treating previous work as foundational to changes about to be made reflects confident and capable leadership. Yet, major overhauls can come with the dismissal of previous work, and sometimes, the dismissal or diminishment of the individuals responsible for that work. At times, such actions are justified, especially if previous curricular decisions were based on faulty research or ill-advised leadership. But, when changes are made in order to simply discount the work of others or distance the institution from earlier efforts, it sends the message that those efforts or the program itself was irrelevant or inconsequential. Failure to adequately consider the contribution of previous efforts may actually delay the integration and adoption of inevitable changes. Further, overly rapid change may reflect poorly on both the institution and the administrator behind the new path.

» Given that most first-year experience initiatives, including first-year seminars, engage a wide array of campus partners, it is important to understand the broad range of effects of first-year seminar change and refinement. When there are changes to the seminar, it can create an imbalance or reaction from other services that have aligned their delivery to support the seminar. It is likely that other programs will need to reconsider their philosophy or approach based on the new actions or expectations of the seminar.

» Maintaining a student centered-approach is as critical to first-year seminar sustainability as it is to understanding the basic tenets of the course (chapter 1) as well as a fundamental theme in the processes of launching, administering, and refining the course (chapters 2-4). In the case of a first-year seminar, it is essential to make decisions about what to teach, how to teach it, and to what ends based upon an assessment of student needs at the institution and the feedback from participants in the seminar at any particular time. This feedback will prove invaluable in efforts to prioritize and deliver those elements that most appropriately address the concerns, issues, and challenges of the students at the institution. As long as the course remains grounded in a student-centered approach, it is much more likely to provide the appropriate levels of challenge and support for first-year students' adjustment to college, seamless matriculation into the second-year, and their ultimate success in higher education.

» In order to remain innovative and focused on improvement, it is important to remain abreast of the newest research, trends, and best practices with respect to first-year seminar delivery and outcomes. An efficient way to keep current on these issues is to become active in the national dialogue on first-year seminars and the first-year experience. This can be achieved by reviewing new publications and periodicals related to the seminar and FYE more broadly; attending statewide, regional, and national professional development events on student success initiatives; becoming engaged in online communities on the seminar and related topics, such as listservs, Facebook groups, and blogging sites; and publishing or presenting assessment findings, research results, and successful strategies from institutional experiences with the seminar. A connection to a larger community of educators who are invested and involved in first-year seminars helps prevent campus personnel from becoming entrenched in institutional habits and history and introduces a steady stream of new ideas to refine and improve the seminar. Appendix A includes a number of resources to help first-year seminar professionals engage with other higher education professionals in the national FYE community.

While not a strict formula for success, consideration of these issues will help maintain ongoing momentum toward effectiveness, relevance, excellence, and ultimately, sustainability of the first-year seminar.

Avoiding Mission Creep and Contextualizing the First-Year Seminar

One of the greatest threats to the relevance and excellence of the first-year seminar is *mission creep*. An interesting term that has been adopted by business and higher education, mission creep originates with the management of military operations. Specifically, it means to take on functions outside of the primary objective. The hazard of too much diversification or expansion into areas other than education results in the sense of being spread too thin or failing to living up to everyone's expectations (Longanecker, 2008). It represents the classic case of trying to provide something for everyone and ultimately providing only a little to a few. The reason for investing in campus partnerships and cultivating broad campus buy-in is to accomplish mission saturation, which is a fully resourced and understood objective by as many members of the campus as possible.

Since first-year seminars reflect the full range of concerns addressed by the campus, it is easy to create a course that becomes, in essence, the homeroom of college. While everyone would have a piece of it, the student learning experience would be diluted by the constant presence of talking heads and announcements. There is little intellectual discovery process in that model, and it lacks the intellectual rigor necessary to qualify for a college course. Thus, it is imperative that the course leadership identifies goals and student learning outcomes that are in line with and support the campus mission. From these elements a strong curriculum can be developed. Thereafter, an ongoing authentic assessment process will ensure that the course remains rooted in these learning outcomes, maintains its relevance and excellence, and effectively contributes to the campus mission.

In order to avoid mission creep, however, it is important to understand that the first-year seminar is not the only tool to provide the challenge and support necessary to facilitate first-year student success. As mentioned in chapter 3, too often higher education professionals and the constituencies they serve, such as students, parents, community partners, alumni, and state legislators, confuse a first-year *seminar* with a first-year *experience* and are, thus, tempted to include an overwhelming amount of content and address too wide a range of student needs in this one curricular intervention. In a new student support model where a seminar is viewed as the only opportunity to educate and introduce first-year students to best practices and educationally purposeful activities, one can easily understand an overzealous effort to make the seminar be everything to everyone. However, anyone who has experienced a transformation, whether it be educational, professional, or personal, knows that an abundance of information that is not appropriately paced or timed for the challenges being faced will feel a bit like a virtual assault of knowledge and fall short of its potential impact. As such, efforts to include every lesson and strategy for success for new students in a first-year seminar is likely to undermine the very goals that the course was developed to achieve. Further, if first-year seminars are equated to a first-year experience, structural limitations, such as one-unit courses or the seminar being offered as an elective, essentially ensure that many students will be cheated of a meaningful first-year experience.

Therefore, it is critical to the ongoing success of the first-year seminar to embrace its limitations as much as its potential. The course is only part of the continuum of services and intentional activities that ensure that students enter the campus in such a way that they can be successful. Indeed, "the first-year experience is not a single program or initiative, but rather an intentional combination of academic and cocurricular efforts within and across postsecondary institutions" (Koch & Gardner, 2006, p. 2). As such, the seminar is one of a number of different opportunities for colleges and universities to facilitate new student learning and success. As addressed throughout this book and in the volumes that follow, the seminar can be effectively linked to several other first-year initiatives. For instance, orientation and welcome week activities are effective precursors to a first-year seminar and often more appropriate programs to communicate information to new students. Academic advising can promote first-year seminar participation, be a course topic, bolster seminar instructional staff, or even represent a requirement of the course. Similarly, developmental education, Supplemental Instruction, and library resources can be effectively woven into the fabric of a first-year seminar, be positioned as structural partners to the course, or represent more effective sources of support for certain new student needs, thereby offering an alternative to achieving those goals within the framework of the course. Frequently, first-year seminars are one of the courses featured in a linked-course, learning community, or living-learning community model. In yet another example, service-learning, experiential education, and information technology are vital components of a rich first-year experience whether or not they are integrated into the content and pedagogy of the seminar. First-year seminars represent just one star in a constellation of curricular and cocurricular programming for first-year student success—a realization that can help avoid the seductive "we must be all things to all people" nature of mission creep.

The notion of intentional integration also goes far beyond the first-year. Although higher education has long identified the first-year as a critical leakage point in the educational pipeline (Pascarella & Terenzini, 1991, 2005; Tinto, 1993; Upcraft et al., 2005), learning and progress do not cease once a student successfully completes his or her first year. In fact, as mentioned in the discussion of learning outcomes in chapter 3, there is often a developmental ceiling to the types of progress that students can achieve in the first year of a major transition as well as at their stage of maturity and development. Therefore, first-year experience initiatives generally, and the first-year seminar specifically, should be structured in such a way as to lay the foundation for educationally and personally meaningful experiences in the second, third, fourth, and fifth years of college and beyond. In other words, first-year experiences, such as the seminar, do not operate in a vacuum but instead must be seen as an integrated component of an educational trajectory. In past decades, the support provided via a first-year seminar, other curricular interventions, and cocurricular initiatives would create a highly encouraging and accommodating first year but leave those same students bereft and longing for institutional attention until they reached the preparations for graduation several years later. More recently, educational researchers and practitioners have started to pay closer attention to student development at other key transition points, such as the sophomore year (Hunter et al., 2010; Tobolowsky & Cox, 2007); the entire senior year (Gardner, Van der Veer, & Associates, 1997); and even the transition into graduate school (Tokuno, 2008), for which the first year sets the precedent. As such, the first-year seminar as a component of the first-year experience represents a key building block of a multiyear educational experience and student success broadly defined.

Closing Thoughts

This volume attempted to achieve several goals. The first chapter offered an introduction to the history, types, and general characteristics of first-year seminars and identified various issues to consider when selecting the appropriate course for a college or university. Chapter 2 described in detail a series of steps for engaging a campus in launching a first-year seminar. The third chapter provided readers with a comprehensive set of points for administering different types of first-year seminars in a variety of institutional contexts. The fourth chapter outlined the forces that create changes for the first-year seminar and included common characteristics of change processes. Finally, a list of references and resources for first-year seminars and course assessment are included in the appendices.

Although this book is intended to be a stand-alone resource for professionals working with first-year seminars, it is difficult to address in depth all of the elements needed for a successful course. Therefore, a secondary goal of this book is to create the foundation for a multivolume series focused on designing, implementing, and assessing first-year seminars. Each subsequent volume will look at a different aspect of seminar design or administration and, similar to this text, offer suggestions for practice grounded in the literature on teaching and learning, research on seminars, and campus-based examples. More specifically, this treatment of the design and administration of a first-year seminar will be followed by books addressing instructor training and development (volume II), teaching strategies in the first-year seminar (volume III), using peers in the first-year seminar classroom (volume IV), and assessment of the seminar (volume V). This series will help serve as a roadmap to continued success for first-year seminars and the students they serve.

Appendix A
Resources on the First-Year Seminar

Periodicals and Essay Series on First-Year Seminars

» *E-Source for College Transitions* (www.sc.edu/fye/esource) is a biannual electronic newsletter published by the National Resource Center for The First-Year Experience and Students in Transition. Its primary purpose is to provide practical strategies for supporting student learning and success.

» *Essays on the First-Year Initiative Benchmarking Study* (www.sc.edu/fye/resources/assessment/essays/Swing-8.28.02.html). The First-Year Initiative (FYI) benchmarking study was launched in fall 2001 to assess and benchmark the learning outcomes of first-year seminars. This series contains essays, study results, and brief reports of key findings.

» *Journal of College Orientation and Transition* (nodaweb.orgsync.com/org/noda/about_journal_of_college_orientation_and_transition), a biannual publication, focuses on the trends, practices, research, and development of programs, policies, and activities related to the matriculation, orientation, transition, and retention of college students. Also encouraged are literature reviews, how-to articles, innovative initiatives, successful practices, and new ideas.

» *Journal of The First-Year Experience & Students in Transition* (www.sc.edu/fye/journal) is a semiannual refereed journal providing current research and scholarship on significant student transitions, including the first college year.

» *The Toolbox* (www.sc.edu/fye/toolbox) is an online professional development newsletter, published six times a year, offering innovative learner-centered strategies for empowering college students to achieve greater success.

Select Publications on First-Year Seminars

Barefoot, B.O., Gardner, J. N., Cutright, M., Morris, L. V., Schroeder, C. C., Schwartz, S. W., . . . Swing, R. L. (2005). *Achieving and sustaining institutional excellence for the first year of college*. San Francisco, CA: Jossey-Bass.

Erickson, B. L., Peters, C. B., & Strommer, D. W. (2006). *Teaching first-year college students*. San Francisco, CA: Jossey-Bass.

Feldman, R. S. (Ed.). (2005). *Improving the first year of college: Research and practice*. Mahwah, NJ: Lawrence Erlbaum Associates.

Gardner, J. N. (1989). Starting a freshman seminar program. In M. L. Upcraft, J. N. Gardner, & Associates, *The freshman year experience* (pp. 238-249). San Francisco, CA: Jossey-Bass.

Griffin, A. M., & Romm, J. (Eds.). (2008). *Exploring the evidence, vol. IV: Reporting research on first-year seminars*. Columbia, SC: University of South Carolina, National Resource Center for The First-Year Experience and Students in Transition. Retrieved from http://www.sc.edu/fye/resources/fyr/index.html

Hunter, M. S., & Linder, C. W. (2005). First-year seminars. In M. L. Upcraft, J. N. Gardner, B. O. Barefoot, & Associates (Eds.), *Challenging and supporting the first-year student: A handbook for improving the first year of college* (pp. 275-291). San Francisco, CA: Jossey-Bass.

Koch, A. K., Foote, S. M., Hinkle, S. E., Keup, J. R., & Pistilli, M. D. (2007). *The first-year experience in American higher education: An annotated bibliography* (Monograph No. 3, 4th ed.). Columbia, SC: University of South Carolina, National Resource Center for The First-Year Experience and Students in Transition.

Tobolowsky, B. F., & Associates. (2008). *2006 National Survey of First-Year Seminars: Continuing innovations in the collegiate curriculum* (Monograph No. 51). Columbia, SC: University of South Carolina, National Resource Center for The First-Year Experience and Students in Transition.

Tobolowsky, B. F., Cox, B. E., & Wagner, M. T. (Eds.). (2005). *Exploring the evidence: Reporting research on first-year seminars, Volume III* (Monograph No. 42). Columbia, SC: University of South Carolina, National Resource Center for The First-Year Experience and Students in Transition.

Associations and Centers Relevant to First-Year Seminars

» *National Resource Center for The First-Year Experience and Students in Transition* (www.sc.edu/fye), located at the University of South Carolina, serves educational professionals by supporting and advancing efforts to improve student learning and transitions into and through higher education. In pursuit of this mission, the Center provides opportunities for the exchange of practical and scholarly information as well as the discussion of trends and issues in higher education through the convening of professional development events, providing a full complement of publications, and a wide variety of online resources, and advancing the research agenda on the first-year experience and students in transition.

» *Association of American Colleges and Universities (AAC&U)* (www.aacu.org) is the leading national association concerned with the quality, vitality, and public standing of undergraduate liberal education. Through its publications, meetings, public advocacy, and programs, AAC&U works to reinforce the commitment to liberal education at both the national and the local levels and to help individual colleges and universities keep the quality of student learning at the core of their work as they evolve to meet new economic and social challenges.

» *John N. Gardner Institute for Excellence in Undergraduate Education* (www.jngi.org) is an organization dedicated to providing information and assistance to enhance college student learning, retention, and ultimately graduation rates. Through its suite of tools and services, including the Foundations of Excellence initiative, the Institute works with postsecondary institutions of different sizes, types, and missions within the United States and in other countries as they evaluate and improve their own policies, practices, and procedures in pursuit of undergraduate excellence. The Institute maintains a special focus on enriching the beginning college experience for both first-time and transfer students.

» *Washington Center for Improving the Quality of Undergraduate Education* (www.evergreen.edu/washcenter/home.asp), located at Evergreen State College, is organized as a consortium, working in collaboration with institutions across the country to share good practices and carry out collaborative projects aimed at improving undergraduate teaching and student learning. Through workshops, institutes, campus visits, publications, and their website, the Washington Center promotes projects aimed at improving student achievement. Notable is its summer institute on developing and sustaining learning communities.

» Several national membership organizations dedicated to certain foci in higher education also have publications, subgroups, committees, recognition programs, and professional opportunities dedicated to FYE and first-year seminars, including

- *Association of College & Research Libraries (ACRL)* a division of the *American Library Association (ALA)* (www.ala.org/acrl)
- *Association of College & University Housing Officers – International (ACUHI-I)* (www.acuho-i.org)
- *Association of Institutional Research (AIR)* (www.airweb.org)
- *Commission for Admissions, Orientation, and First Year Experience in ACPA, College Student Educators International* (www.myacpa.org/comm/aofye/index.cfm);
- *National Association of Student Personnel Administrators (NASPA)* (www.naspa.org)
- *National Academic Advising Association (NACADA)* (www.nacada.ksu.edu/)
- *National Orientation Directors Association (NODA)* (noda.orgsync.com).

Professional Development Opportunities Related to First-Year Seminars

» *National and International Conferences on The First-Year Experience*
- *Annual Conference on The First-Year Experience* is sponsored by the National Resource Center for The First-Year Experience and Students in Transition and represents the premier, comprehensive professional development event in the United States dedicated to the transition, learning, adjustment, and success of first-year students, including the latest research, assessment, trends, and issues on first-year seminars.
- *International Conference on The First-Year Experience* is sponsored by the National Resource Center for The First-Year Experience and Students in Transition and provides a forum for sharing ideas, concepts, resources, programmatic interventions, and research results focused on the first-year of college or university with institutions and educators across the globe.
- *European Conference on the First Year Experience* is a relatively young conference that explores the student experience at institutions of higher education across Europe, with a specific focus on the importance of the first year. By sharing good practices, getting acquainted with innovative

actions to support student learning, and introducing new research, it seeks to empower educators to improve the quality of European higher education.

- *Pacific Rim First Year in Higher Education Conference* has provided the opportunity to disseminate research and practice for enhancing the first year in higher education in Australasia on an annual basis for more than a decade. The presentations at this conference address the latest scholarship and practice on a number of topics relevant to the first-year experience, such as pedagogy, diversity, partnerships, assessment, equity issues, and technology.

» *Regional and institutional conferences* draw from regional interest groups, collaboratives, and individual institutions to hold conferences, often single-day, drive-in meetings, focused on specific aspects of the first-year experience.

» *Disciplinary conferences.* Every discipline has first-year students, and many professional associations sponsor opportunities for faculty members to consider the implications of introducing the discipline to new students.

» *Institutes* offer opportunities to look at first-year seminars and related topics in greater depth and create strategies and action plans for implementation and improvement. Prominent examples include

- *Institute for First-Year Seminar Leadership* sponsored by the National Resource Center for The First-Year Experience and Students in Transition

- *National Summer Institute for Learning Communities* hosted by the Washington Center for Improving the Quality of Undergraduate Education

- *Summer Institutes* held by AAC&U

» *Webinars, online courses, and distance learning experiences* sponsored by for-profit and not-for-profit entities can serve as resources for training events or initiatives focused on improving a first-year experience program.

Other Resources on First-Year Seminars

» *University 101 Programs Faculty Resource Manual* was designed by the University 101 staff and campus partners at the University of South Carolina and provides instructional faculty with a guide to design, manage, teach, and assess the first-year seminar. Although institution-specific, the content provides a comprehensive example of instructional elements for an award-winning first-year seminar program.

» *Publishers* invested in providing textbooks and ancillary materials to support the teaching of first-year seminars will host conferences, round table discussions and focus groups at other conferences, or specially tailored workshops to assist faculty when using their materials.

» *Listservs,* most notably the first-year experience (FYE) listserv sponsored by the National Resource Center for The First-Year Experience and Students in Transition, offer easy access to a national dialogue on all FYE topics and often include conversations and posts regarding first-year seminars.

» *Facebook pages* are available for many of the organizations dedicated to the first-year experience and first-year seminars and provide a network as well as a gateway for important information about professional development events, blogs, and other opportunities.

» *The First-Year Resources Page* hosted by the National Resource Center for The First-Year Experience and Students in Transition (www.sc.edu/fye/resources/fyr) is a repository of information and examples of the first-year seminar from campuses and programs across the country, which includes sample syllabi, program descriptions, common reading selections, and position descriptions for professional positions related to the first-year seminar.

Appendix B
Resources on Assessment of the First-Year Seminar

Periodicals Relevant to Assessment of First-Year Seminars

» *Assessment Update* (onlinelibrary.wiley.com/journal/10.1002 (ISSN)1536-0725) is a bimonthly newsletter published by Wiley and distributed by the Association of Institutional Research, which is dedicated to covering the latest developments in higher education assessment. *Assessment Update* offers all academic leaders with up-to-date information and practical advice on conducting assessments in a range of areas, including student learning and outcomes, faculty instruction, academic programs and curricula, student services, and overall institutional functioning.

» *New Directions in Institutional Research* (onlinelibrary.wiley.com/journal/10.1002/(ISSN)1536-075X) is a publication series published by Wiley that focuses on providing planners and administrators in all types of academic institutions with guidelines in such areas as resource coordination, information analysis, program evaluation, and institutional management.

» *Research in Higher Education* (www.springerlink.com/content/101599/) is a scholarly journal that is published eight times a year by the Association of Institutional Research with the purpose of disseminating scholarly works that contribute to the collective understanding of one or more institutions of higher education in order to aid faculty and administrators to make informed decisions, and to improve efficiency or effectiveness.

Select Publications Related to Assessment of First-Year Seminars

Astin, A.W. (1991). *Assessment for excellence: The philosophy and practice of assessment and evaluation in higher education.* Phoenix, AZ: American Council on Education/Oryx Press.

Bresciani, M. J. (2006). *Outcomes-based academic and co-curricular program review.* Sterling, VA: Stylus.

Gahagan, J., Dingfelder, J., & Pei, K. (2010). *A faculty and staff guide to creating learning outcomes.* Columbia, SC: University of South Carolina, National Resource Center for The First-Year Experience and Students in Transition.

Maki, P. L. (2004). *Assessing for learning: Building a sustainable commitment across the institution.* Sterling, VA: Stylus.

Palomba, C. A., & Banta, T. W. (1999). *Assessment essentials.* San Francisco, CA: Jossey-Bass.

Suskie, L. (2009). *Assessing student learning.* San Francisco, CA: Jossey-Bass.

Swing, R. L., & Upcraft, M. L. (2005). Choosing and using assessment instruments. In M. L. Upcraft, J. N. Gardner, B. O. Barefoot, & Associates, *Challenging and supporting the first-year student: A handbook for improving the first year of college* (pp. 501-514). San Francisco, CA: Jossey-Bass.

Tobolowsky, B. F., Cox, B. E., & Wagner, M. T. (Eds.). (2005). *Exploring the evidence: Reporting research on first-year seminars, Volume III* (Monograph No. 42). Columbia, SC: University of South Carolina, National Resource Center for The First-Year Experience and Students in Transition.

Upcraft, M. L. (2005). Assessing the first-year of college. In M. L. Upcraft, J. N. Gardner, B. O. Barefoot, & Associates, *Challenging and supporting the first-year student: A handbook for improving the first year of college* (pp. 469-485). San Francisco, CA: Jossey-Bass.

Upcraft, M. L., Crissman Ishler, J. L., & Swing, R. L. (2005). A beginner's guide for assessing the first college year. In M. L. Upcraft, J. N. Gardner, B. O. Barefoot, & Associates, *Challenging and supporting the first-year student: A handbook for improving the first year of college* (pp. 486-500). San Francisco, CA: Jossey-Bass.

Upcraft, M. L., & Schuh, J. H. (1996). *Assessment in student affairs: A guide for practitioners.* San Francisco, CA: Jossey-Bass.

Winston, R. B., & Miller, T. K. (1994). A model for assessing developmental outcomes related to student affairs programs and services. *NASPA Journal, 32*(1), 2-19.

Select Associations and Centers Relevant to the Assessment and Research of First-Year Seminars

» *Higher Education Research Institute (HERI)* (www.heri.ucla.edu), located at the University of California, Los Angeles, seeks to inform educational policy and promote institutional improvement through an increased understanding of higher education and its impact on college students. In pursuit of this mission, HERI provides tools and resources to conduct research on student transition and college impact at the institutional level—including the Cooperative Institutional Research Program (CIRP) Freshman Survey, Your First College Year (YFCY) survey, and College Senior Survey—and advances an original research agenda on these topics using national data.

» *Educational Benchmarking, Inc. (EBI)* (www.webebi.com) aims to provide comprehensive, comparative assessment instruments and analysis to support quality improvement efforts on institutional and student issues, such as housing, student activities, Greek life, and various academic programs. The First-Year Initiative (FYI) Seminar Assessment is administered at the end of first-year seminar and provides feedback regarding course outcomes. Studies using national samples of data collected via this survey have advanced the greater understanding of first-year seminar impact on student outcomes.

» *The Center for Postsecondary Research*, located at Indiana University, is the home of the National Survey of Student Engagement (NSSE) (nsse.iub.edu), which collects information annually at hundreds of four-year colleges and universities about student participation in programs and activities, including first-year seminars, that institutions provide for their learning and personal development. These data can be used to identify aspects of the undergraduate experience inside and outside the classroom that can be improved through changes in policies and initiatives more consistent with good practices in undergraduate education.

» *The Community College Survey of Student Engagement* (CCSSE) (www.ccsse.org/) is housed at the Community College Leadership Program at The University of Texas at Austin and works in partnership with the National Survey of Student Engagement (NSSE). Designed to address the unique missions of community colleges and the characteristics of their diverse student populations, CCSSE's survey instrument, The Community College Student Report, provides information on student engagement at two-year colleges. The survey, administered to thousands of community college students each year, asks questions that assess institutional practices and student behaviors that are highly correlated with student learning and student retention. The data generated by this national instrument can be used as a benchmarking instrument, diagnostic tool, and a monitoring device for student engagement, learning, and success as well as institutional quality.

Other Resources on Assessment of First-Year Seminars

» *Listservs,* most notably the first-year assessment (FYA) listserv sponsored by the National Resource Center for The First-Year Experience and Students in Transition, offer easy access to a national dialogue on the assessment of FYE topics and often include conversations and posts regarding the evaluation of first-year seminars.

» The *Assessment Resources Page* of the website for the National Resource Center for The First-Year Experience and Students in Transition (www.sc.edu/fye/resources/assessment) includes a variety of resources related to the assessment of first-year seminars and new student experiences, such as an overview of assessment in the first college year, a typology and database of commercially available and relevant assessment instruments, examples of locally developed surveys, invited essays on first-year assessment from national experts, and related research findings on FYE and first-year seminars.

References

American Association for Higher Education (AAHE), American College Personnel Association (ACPA), & National Association of Student Personnel Administrators (NASPA). (1998). *Powerful partnerships: A shared responsibility for learning.* Washington, DC: Author.

American College Testing. (2009). *Retention/completion summary tables.* Retrieved from the ACT website: http://www.act.org/research/policymakers/reports/graduation.html

American College Testing. (2010). *National collegiate retention and persistence to degree rates.* Retrieved from the ACT website: http://www.act.org/research/policymakers/reports/graduation.html

Arries, J. F. (1999). Critical pedagogy and service-learning in Spanish: Crossing borders in the freshman seminar. In J. Hellebrandt & L. T. Varona (Eds.), *Construyendo puentes (building bridges): Concepts and models for service-learning in Spanish* (pp. 33-47). Washington, DC: American Association for Higher Education.

Astin, A. (1984). Student involvement: A developmental theory for higher education. *Journal of College Student Personnel, 25,* 297-308.

Astin, A. W. (1993). *What matters in college? Four critical years revisited.* San Francisco, CA: Jossey-Bass.

Astin, A. W., & Oseguera, L. (2005). *Degree attainment rates at American colleges and universities* (Revised ed.). Los Angeles, CA: University of California, Los Angeles, Higher Education Research Institute.

Barefoot, B. O. (1992). *Helping first-year college students climb the academic ladder: Report of a national survey of freshman seminar programming in American higher education.* (Unpublished doctoral dissertation). College of William and Mary, Williamsburg, VA.

Barefoot, B. O. (2002). *2002 National Survey of First-Year Academic Practices Findings.* Brevard, NC: Policy Center on the First Year of College. Retrieved from the John N. Gardner Institute for Excellence in Undergraduate Education website: http://www.jngi.org/2002nationalsurvey

Barefoot, B. O., & Fidler, P. P. (1996). An historic and theoretical framework for the freshman seminar. In *The 1994 national survey of freshman seminar programs: Continuing innovations in the collegiate curriculum* (Monograph No. 20, pp. 5-9). Columbia, SC: University of South Carolina, National Resource Center for The Freshman Year Experience and Students in Transition.

Barefoot, B. O., Gardner, J. N., Cutright, M., Morris, L. V., Schroeder, C. C., Schwartz, S. W., … & Swing, R. L. (2005). *Achieving and sustaining institutional excellence for the first year of college.* San Francisco, CA: Jossey-Bass.

Barefoot, B. O., Warnock, C. L., Dickinson, M. P., Richardson, S. E., & Roberts, M. R. (Eds.). (1998). *Exploring the evidence: Reporting research on first-year seminars, Volume II* (Monograph No. 25). Columbia, SC: University of South Carolina, National Resource Center for The First-Year Experience and Students in Transition.

Bauer, K. W. (2003). Assessment for institutional research: Guidelines and resources. In W. E. Knight (Ed.), *The primer for institutional research* (pp. 9-23). Tallahassee, FL: Association for Institutional Research.

Baxter Magolda, M. B. (1999). Engaging students in active learning. In G. S. Blimling & E. J. Whitt (Eds.), *Good practice in student affairs: Principles to foster student learning* (pp. 21-43). San Francisco, CA: Jossey-Bass.

Bedford, M. H., & Durkee, P. E. (1989). Retention: Some more ideas. *NASPA Journal, 27,* 168-171.

Beil, C., & Knight, M. A. (2007). Understanding the gap between high school and college writing. *Assessment Update, 19*(6), 6-8.

Boyce, M. E. (2003). Organizational learning is essential to achieving and sustaining change in higher education. *Innovative Higher Education, 28*(2), 119-136.

Braxton, J. M., Milem, J. F., & Sullivan, A. S. (2000). The influence of active learning on the college student departure process. *The Journal of Higher Education, 71*(5), 569-590.

Campbell, D. (2006, fall). Keeping them in college: East Carolina University's efforts to improve retention and graduation rates. *National Crosstalk, 1,* 14-16.

Cavote, S. E., & Kopera-Frye, K. (2004). Subject-based first-year experience courses: Questions about program effectiveness. *Journal of The First-Year Experience & Students in Transition, 16*(2), 85-102.

Centra, J. A., & Gaubatz, N. B. (2005). *Student perceptions of learning and instructional effectiveness in college courses: A validity study of SIRII.* Princeton, NJ: Educational Testing Service.

Chickering, A.W., & Gamson, Z. F. (1987). Seven principles for good practice in undergraduate education. *AAHE Bulletin, 39*(7), 3-6.

Cohen, A. M., & Kisker, C.B. (2010). *The shaping of American higher education: Emergence and growth of the contemporary system* (2nd ed.). San Francisco, CA: Jossey-Bass.

Collins, J. C. (2001). *From good to great: Why some companies make it and others don't.* New York, NY: HarperCollins.

Crissman Ishler, J. L. (2005). Today's first-year students. In M. L. Upcraft, J. N. Gardner, B. O. Barefoot, & Associates, *Challenging and supporting the first-year student: A handbook for improving the first year of college* (pp. 15-26). San Francisco, CA: Jossey-Bass.

Cronbach, L. J., & Snow, R. E. (1977). *Aptitudes and instructional methods: A handbook for research on interactions.* New York, NY: Irvington Publishers.

Cuseo, J. B. (1991). *The freshman orientation seminar: A research-based rationale for its value, delivery, and content* (Monograph No. 4). Columbia, SC: University of South Carolina, National Resource Center for The Freshman Year Experience.

Donahue, L. (2004). Connections and reflections: Creating a positive learning environment for first year students. *Journal of The First Year Experience & Students in Transition, 16*(1), 77-100.

Duranczyk, I. M., & White, W. G. (Eds.). (2003). *Developmental education: Pathways to excellence.* Findlay, OH: National Association for Developmental Education. Retrieved from NADE website: http://www.nade.net/publications/monograph.html

Engberg, M. E., & Mayhew, M. J. (2007). The influences of student "success" courses on student learning and democratic outcomes. *Journal of College Student Development, 48*(3), 241-258.

Erickson, B. L., & Strommer, D. W. (1991). *Teaching college freshmen.* San Francisco, CA: Jossey-Bass.

Erickson, B. L., Peters, C. B., & Strommer, D. W. (2006). *Teaching first-year college students.* San Francisco, CA: Jossey-Bass.

Evans, N. J., Forney, D. S., & Guido-DiBrito, F. (1998). *Student development in college: Theory, research, and practice.* San Francisco, CA: Jossey-Bass.

Fidler, P. P. (1991). Relationship of freshman orientation seminars to sophomore return rates. *Journal of The Freshman Year Experience, 3*(1), 7-38.

Fidler, P. P., & Moore, P. S. (1996). A comparison of effects of campus residence and freshman seminar attendance on freshman dropout rates. *Journal of The Freshman Year Experience & Students in Transition, 8*(2), 7-16.

Fidler, P. P., Neururer-Rotholz, J., & Richardson, S. (1999). Teaching the freshman seminar: Its effectiveness in promoting faculty development. *Journal of The First-Year Experience & Student in Transition, 11*(2), 59-74.

Friedman, D. (2009, April 19). *Ensuring relevance and excellence.* Institute for First-Year Seminar Leadership, Asheville, NC.

Friedman, D., & Marsh, E. (2009). What type of freshman seminar is most effective? A Comparison of thematic seminars and college transition/success seminars. *Journal of The First-Year Experience & Students in Transition, 21*(1) 29-42.

Gahagan, J. S. (2002). A historical and theoretical framework for the first-year seminar. In *2000 National Survey of First-Year Seminar Programs: Continuing innovations in the collegiate curriculum* (Monograph No. 35, pp. 11-76). Columbia, SC: University of South Carolina, National Resource Center for The First-Year Experience and Students in Transition.

Gahagan, J., Dingfelder, J., & Pei, K (2010). *A faculty and staff guide to creating learning outcomes.* Columbia, SC: University of South Carolina, National Resource Center for The First-Year Experience and Students in Transition.

Gallagher, R. P. (2004). *National Survey of Counseling Center Directors.* Pittsburgh, PA: International Association of Counseling Services.

Gardner, J. N., Van der Veer, G., & Associates. (1997). *The senior year experience: Facilitating integration, reflection, closure, and transition.* San Francisco, CA: Jossey-Bass.

General Education Task Force. (2007, May 9). *Final report.* Retrieved from Appalachian State University website: http://www.generaleducation.appstate.edu/general-education-task-force-report

Gladwell, M. (2000). *The tipping point: How little things can make a big difference.* New York, NY: Little, Brown.

Gilchrist, D. (2007) *Improving student experience: Assessment-as-learning.* [Illinois Immersion Program Participant Notebook]. ACRL Institute for Information Literacy, Chicago, IL.

Goodwin, L. C., & Schuker, D. J. T. (2006, April 19). College turnover troubles profs: New staff bring "fresh ideas," but some faculty miss familiar faces. *The Harvard Crimson.* Retrieved from the Harvard Crimson website: http://www.thecrimson.com/article/2006/4/19/college-turnover-troubles-profs-in-his/

Griffin, A. M., & Romm, J. (Eds.). (2008). *Exploring the evidence: Reporting research on first-year seminars, vol. IV.* Columbia, SC: University of South Carolina, National Resource Center for The First-Year Experience and Students in Transition. Retrieved from http://www.sc.edu/fye/resources/fyr/index.html

Hamid, S. (2001). *Peer leadership: A primer for program essentials* (Monograph No. 32). Columbia, SC: University of South Carolina, National Resource Center for The First-Year Experience and Students in Transition.

Henscheid, J. M. (2004). First-year seminars in learning communities: Two reforms intersect. In J. M. Henscheid (Ed.), *Integrating the first-year experience: The role of first-year seminars in learning communities* (Monograph No. 39, pp. 1-7). Columbia, SC: University of South Carolina, National Resource Center for The First-Year Experience and Students in Transition.

Hoffman, M., Richmond, J., Morrow, J., & Salomone, K. (2002-2003). Investigating "sense of belonging" in first-year college students. *Journal of College Student Retention: Research, Theory, & Practice, 4*(3), 227-256.

Hopkins, W. H. (1988). *College success: A transitional course for freshmen.* Washington, DC: American Association of State Colleges and Universities.

Hunter, M. S., & Linder, C. W. (2005). First-year seminars. In M. L. Upcraft, J. N. Gardner, B. O. Barefoot, & Associates, *Challenging and supporting the first-year student: A handbook for improving the first year of college* (pp. 275-291). San Francisco, CA: Jossey-Bass.

Hunter, M. S., & Skipper, T. L. (Eds.). (1999). *Solid foundations: Building success for first-year seminars through instructor training and development* (Monograph No. 29). Columbia, SC: University of South Carolina, National Resource Center for The First-Year Experience and Students in Transition.

Hunter. M. S., Tobolowsky, B. F., Gardner, J. N., Evenbeck, S. E., Pattengale, J. A., Schaller, M., & Schreiner, L. A. (2010). *Helping sophomores succeed: Understanding and improving the second-year experience.* San Francisco, CA: Jossey-Bass.

Kain, D. J. (2003). Teacher-centered versus student-centered: Balancing constraint and theory in the composition classroom. *Pedagogy, 3*(1), 104-108.

Keeling, R. P., Underhile, R., & Wall, A. F. (2007). Horizontal and vertical structures: The dynamics of organizations in higher education. *Liberal Education, 93*(4), 22-31.

Keup, J. R., & Barefoot, B. O. (2005). Learning how to be a successful student: Exploring the impact of first-year seminars on student outcomes. *Journal of The First-Year Experience & Students in Transition, 17*(1), 11-47.

Keup, J. R., & Mullins, E. (2010, February). *Findings from a national survey of peer leadership experiences and outcomes.* 29th Annual Conference on The First-Year Experience, Denver, CO.

Kezar, A. (2002). Organizational models and facilitators of change: Providing a framework for student and academic affairs collaboration. In A. Kezar, D. Hirsch, & C. Burack (Eds.), *Understanding the role of academic and student affairs collaboration in creating a successful learning environment* (New Directions for Higher Education No. 116, pp. 63-74). San Francisco, CA: Jossey-Bass.

King, P. M., & Baxter Magolda, M. B. (2005). A developmental model of intercultural maturity. *Journal of College Student Development, 46*(6), 571-592.

King, P. M., & Kitchener, K. S. (1994). *Developing reflective judgment: Understanding and promoting intellectual growth and critical thinking in adolescents and adults.* San Francisco, CA: Jossey-Bass.

Koch, A. K. (2001). *The first-year experience in American higher education: An annotated bibliography* (Monograph No. 3, 3rd ed.). Columbia, SC: University of South Carolina, National Resource Center for The First-Year Experience & Students in Transition.

Koch, A. K., Foote, S. M., Hinkle, S. E., Keup, J. R., & Pistilli, M. D. (2007). *The first-year experience in American higher education: An annotated bibliography* (Monograph No. 3, 4th ed.). Columbia, SC: University of South Carolina, National Resource Center for The First-Year Experience and Students in Transition.

Koch, A. K., & Gardner, J. N. (2006). The history of the first-year experience in the United States: Lessons from the past, practices in the present, and implications for the future. In A. Hamana & K. Tatsuo (Eds.), *The first-year experience and transition from high school to college: An international study of content and pedagogy.* Tokyo, Japan: Maruzen Publishing.

Kotter, J. (1995. March-April). Leading change: Why transformation efforts fail. *Harvard Business Review, 59-67*.

Kotter, J. (1996). *Leading change*. Boston, MA: Harvard Business School Press.

Kuh, G. (2005). Student engagement in the first year of college. In M. L. Upcraft, J. N. Gardner, & B. O. Barefoot (Eds.), *Challenging and supporting the first-year student: A handbook for improving the first year of college* (pp. 86-107). San Francisco, CA: Jossey-Bass.

Kuh, G. D., Kinzie, J. I., Schuh, J. H., Whitt, E. J., & Associates. (2005). *Student success in college: Creating conditions that matter*. San Francisco, CA: Jossey-Bass.

Kuh, G. D., Schuh, J. H., Whitt, E. J., & Associates. (1991). *Involving colleges: Successful approaches to fostering student learning and development outside the classroom*. San Francisco, CA: Jossey-Bass.

Kuh, G. D., & Whitt, E. J. (1988). *The invisible tapestry: Culture in American colleges and universities* (ASHE-ERIC Higher Education Report Volume 17, No. 1). Washington, DC: The George Washington University Graduate School of Education and Human Development.

Light, R. J. (2001). *Making the most of college: Students speak their minds*. Cambridge, MA: Harvard University Press.

Longanecker, D. A. (2008). *Mission differentiation versus mission creep: Higher education's battle between creationism and evolution*, (Policy Brief for National Conference of State Legislatures and the Western Interstate Commission for Higher Education). Boulder, CO: WICHE.

Liu, A., Sharkness, J., & Pryor, J. H. (2008). *Findings from the 2007 administration of Your First College Year (YFCY): National aggregates*. Los Angeles, CA: University of California, Los Angeles, Higher Education Research Institute.

MacDonald, M. C., & Izenstark, A. K. (2008, May). *Reduce, reuse, recycle: Revamping a freshman seminar information literacy program*. Presentation at 2008 LOEX Annual Conference, Oak Brook, IL.

Maisto, A. A., & Tammi, M. W. (1991). The effect of a content-based freshman seminar on academic and social integration. *Journal of The Freshman Year Experience, 3*(2), 29-48.

Maki, P. L. (2004). *Assessing for learning: Building a sustainable commitment across the institution*. Sterling, VA: Stylus.

Mandel, R. G., & Evans, K. (2003, March/April). First choice: Creating innovative academic options for first-year students. *About Campus, 8*, 23-26.

McGhee, P. (2003). *The academic quality handbook: Enhancing higher education in universities and further education colleges*. Routledge, UK: Taylor & Francis Group.

Merkel, C. A. (2001, May 1). *Undergraduate research at six research universities: A pilot study for the Association of American Universities*. Pasadena, CA: California Institute of Technology.

National Center for Education Statistics. (2009). *Projections of education statistics to 2018, NCES 2009-062.* Washington, DC: U.S. Department of Education.

National Survey of Student Engagement (NSSE). (2008). *Promoting engagement for all students: The imperative to look within.* Bloomington, IN: Indiana University Center for Postsecondary Research.

National Survey of Student Engagement (NSSE). (2009). *Assessment for improvement: Tracking student engagement over time—Annual results 2009.* Bloomington, IN: Indiana University Center for Postsecondary Research.

Pace, C. R. (1984). *Measuring the quality of college student experiences: An account of the development and use of the College Student Experiences Questionnaire.* Los Angeles, CA: University of California, Los Angeles, Higher Education Research Institute. (ERIC Document Reproduction Services No. ED 255099)

Padgett, R. D., & Keup, J. R. (in press). *2009 National Survey of First-Year Seminars: Ongoing efforts to support students in transition* (Research Reports on College Transitions No. 2). Columbia, SC: University of South Carolina, National Resource Center for The First-Year Experience and Students in Transition.

Palomba, C. A., & Banta, T. W. (1999). *Assessment essentials: Planning, implementing, and improving assessment in higher education.* San Francisco, CA: Jossey-Bass.

Pascarella, E. T. (2006). How college affects students: Ten directions for future research. *Journal of College Student Development, 47*(5), 508-520.

Pascarella, E. T., & Terenzini, P. T. (1991). *How college affects students.* San Francisco, CA: Jossey-Bass.

Pascarella, E. T., & Terenzini, P. T. (2005). *How college affects students, Vol. 2: A third decade of research.* San Francisco, CA: Jossey-Bass.

Price, J., & Ferreri, E. (2009, September 5). UNC system struggles with cuts. *News and Observer.* Retrieved from University of North Carolina Central website: http://nccueagles.yuku.com/topic/4881/UNC--struggles--cuts-Campuses--171-million

Pryor, J. H., Hurtado, S., DeAngelo, L., Palucki Blake, L., & Tran, S. (2009). *The American freshman: National norms fall 2009.* Los Angeles, CA: University of California, Los Angeles, Higher Education Research Institute.

Pryor, J. H., Hurtado, S., Saenz, V. B., Santos, J. L., & Korn, W. S. (2007). *The American freshman: Forty-year trends.* Los Angeles, CA: University of California, Los Angeles, Higher Education Research Institute.

Sanoff, A. P. (2006, March 10). What professors and teachers think: A perception gap over students' preparation. *Chronicle of Higher Education,* p. B9.

Saunders, D. F., & Romm, J. (2008). An historical perspective on first-year seminars. In B. F. Tobolowsky & Associates, *2006 National Survey of First-Year Seminars: Continuing innovations in the collegiate curriculum* (Monograph No. 51, pp. 1-3). Columbia, SC: University of South Carolina, National Resource Center for The First-Year Experience and Students in Transition.

Schein, E. H. (1992). *Organizational culture and leadership* (2nd ed.). San Francisco, CA: Jossey-Bass.

Schnell, C. A., & Doetkott, C. (2002-3). First-year seminars produce long-term impact. *Journal of College Student Retention: Research, Theory, & Practice, 4*(4), 377-391.

Schroeder, C. C. (1999). Forging educational partnerships that advance student learning. In G. S. Blimling & E. J. Whitt (Eds.), *Good practice in student affairs: Principles to foster student learning* (pp. 133-156). San Francisco, CA: Jossey-Bass.

Schroeder, C.C. (2003, September/October). The first year and beyond: Charles Schroder talks to John Gardner. *About Campus, 8,* 9-17.

Schroeder, C. C., Minor, F., & Tarkow, T. (1999). Learning communities: Partnerships between academic and student affairs. In, J. H. Levine (Ed.), *Learning communities: New structures, new partnerships for learning* (Monograph No. 26, pp. 59-66). Columbia, SC: University of South Carolina, National Resource Center for The First-Year Experience and Students in Transition.

Sloop, J., Berquist, F., Jones, Y., Moore, R., Thompson, M., Collins, W., Ellingham, M., ...& Bremer, J. (2004-2005). *Achieving eXcellence in liberal education.* Nashville, TN: Vanderbilt University.

Starke, M. C., Harth, M., & Sirianni, F. (2001). Retention, bonding, and academic achievement: Success of a first-year seminar. *Journal of The First-Year Experience & Students in Transition, 13*(2), 7-35.

Subrahmanyam, D. (2009, April 23). Seminar offices combine forces. *Yale Daily News.* Retrieved from Yale Daily News website: http://www.yaledailynews.com/news/2009/apr/23/seminar-offices-combine-forces/

Swing, R. L. (2002). *Series of essays on the First-Year Initiative Benchmarking Study.* Brevard, NC: Policy Center on the First Year of College. Retrieved from the National Resource Center for The First-Year Experience and Students in Transition website: http://www.sc.edu/fye/resources/assessment/essays/Swing-8.28.02.html

Tinto, V. (1993). *Leaving college: Rethinking the causes and cures of student attrition* (2nd ed.). Chicago, IL: University of Chicago Press.

Tobolowsky, B. F., & Associates (2008). *2006 National Survey of First-Year Seminars: Continuing innovations in the collegiate curriculum* (Monograph No. 51). Columbia, SC: University of South Carolina, National Resource Center for The First-Year Experience and Students in Transition.

Tobolowsky, B. F., & Cox, B. E. (2007). *Shedding light on sophomores: An exploration of the second college year* (Monograph No. 47). Columbia, SC: University of South Carolina, National Resource Center for The First-Year Experience and Students in Transition.

Tobolowsky, B. F., Cox, B. E., & Wagner, M. T. (Eds.). (2005). *Exploring the evidence: Reporting research on first-year seminars, Volume III* (Monograph No. 42). Columbia, SC: University of South Carolina, National Resource Center for The First-Year Experience and Students in Transition.

Tokuno, K. A. (Ed.). (2008). *Graduate students in transition: Assisting students through the first year* (Monograph No. 50). Columbia, SC: University of South Carolina, National Resource Center for The First-Year Experience & Students in Transition.

Upcraft, M. L., Gardner, J. N., Barefoot, B. O., & Associates. (2005). *Challenging and supporting the first-year student: A handbook for improving the first year of college.* San Francisco, CA: Jossey-Bass.

Weimer, M. (2002). *Learner-centered teaching: Five key changes to practice.* San Francisco, CA: Jossey-Bass.

Western Interstate Commission for Higher Education. (2008). *Knocking at the college door: Projections of high school graduates by state and race/ethnicity 1992-2022.* Boulder, CO: Author.

Whitt, E. J., Nesheim, B. E., Buentzel, M. J., Kellogg, A. H., McDonald, W. M., & Wells, C. A. (2008). "Principles of good practice" for academic and student affairs partnership programs. *Journal of College Student Development, 49*(3), 235-249.

Zlotkowski, E. (2005). Service-learning and the first-year student. In M. L. Upcraft, J. N. Gardner, B. O. Barefoot, & Associates, *Challenging and supporting the first-year student: A handbook for improving the first year of college* (pp. 256-370). San Francisco, CA: Jossey-Bass.

Index

NOTE: Page numbers with italicized *f* or *t* indicate *figures* or *tables* respectively.

F

O

P

About the Authors

Jennifer R. Keup is the director of the National Resource Center for The First-Year Experience and Students in Transition at the University of South Carolina, where she is responsible for operational and strategic aspects of the Center. Before joining the staff of the National Resource Center, Keup had professional roles in the national dialogue on the first-year experience as well as higher education research and assessment as a project director at the Higher Education Research Institute and was heavily involved in institutional assessment efforts as the director of the Student Affairs Information and Research Office (SAIRO) at the University of California – Los Angeles. Her research interests focus on students' personal and academic development during the transition from high school to college; the influence of campus programming on adjustment to college; and issues of institutional impact, responsiveness, and transformation in higher education.

Joni Webb Petschauer has 25 years of experience in working with college access and success programs. She taught in Appalachian State University's Freshman Seminar program for 18 years and was responsible for administering the implementation of the Freshman Learning Communities program on that campus. Additionally, Petschauer was engaged in faculty development efforts for both programs. Recently retired from the University, she continues to serve as a program evaluator and faculty development workshop leader while writing about student success practices in the United States.